D0595100

the working woman's guide to

BALANCING KIDS, CAREER, HOUSE AND SPOUSE

or, If there is a light at the end of the tunnel it's probably a fire.

Mimi O'Bara

Gráinne Enterprises
Manchester, Massachusetts

Copyright © 2002 by Mimi O'Bara

All rights reserved. No part of this book may be reproduced
or transmitted in any form or by any means, electronic
or mechanical, including photocopying, recording, or by
any information storage and retrival system, without
permission in writing from the publisher.

Published by Gráinne Enterprises,
Manchester, Massachusetts
www.mimi-o'bara.com

Printed in Canada

Design by Cassandra R. Smith
CRS Design

Library of Congress Cataloging-in-Publication Data
O'Bara, Mimi
the working woman's guide to
BALANCING KIDS AND CAREER
HOUSE AND SPOUSE — 1st ed.
2002100621

ISBN 0-9716660-0-8

I would like to dedicate this book to all of those who were injured or lost their lives in the terrorist attacks on the United States of America, on September 11, 2001. At the time of these terrorist attacks, I was in Ireland, taking time away from my family and my job, to do research for and to write this book.

As I attempted to absorb and digest the unfathomable news, I was first devastated, then paralyzed. I crumbled under the weight of the grief and pain of the events and found myself unable to write; consumed by the need to get home and be with my family.

Then, Rudy Giuliani, the mayor of New York City came on CNN and said that it was important for all of us to send a message to the terrorists that they will neither stop us nor will they slow us down. He encouraged all Americans, but specifically all New Yorkers, to show these despicable individuals that they may bend us, but we will never break. With that message, I went back to my computer and continued to write this book, inspired by my sympathy for each of those people who were injured or lost their lives, as well as their families and my immeasurable rage at the deep seated hatred that exists in the souls of those who orchestrated and executed this tragedy.

My hope is that we will all remain acutely aware that each day, as we get out of bed, an event may occur during that day which we could never anticipate but will forever change the landscape of our lives. I hope that I can harness everything I am feeling now and never forget to treat those I love generously and with great compassion, be ready to forgive and forget, and, most importantly, never leave them with an angry word.

God bless America.

Thank You, Thank You, Thank You

As I tried to steal a Saturday afternoon or the random Thursday evening to write this book, it soon became apparent to me that it would not get written unless I was able to isolate myself from the demands of my family and my job. I was fortunate enough to be able to go to Cashel House, a wonderful hotel located in one of the most beautiful places in the world, the rocky coast of Connemara, Co. Galway, Ireland. The proprietors are the McEvilly family, the most warm and welcoming hosts I have ever encountered. The Cashel House grounds and gardens are breathtaking, the rustic beauty of the Connemara ocean and mountains are a view of which I could never tire. It was in these peaceful surroundings that I wrote this book. By the way, don't let anyone tell you that the food in Ireland is sub par. Each evening a fabulous five course meal is served in the dining room, the breakfasts go on forever and afternoon tea is delightful. If you are lucky enough to find yourself in Ireland, do yourself a favor and go up to Cashel House, I can guarantee that you will not be disappointed. And please, extend the McEvillys my warmest regards.

I would like to thank all of my friends who have shared their stories with me over the years and encouraged me to write this book. Thanks for all of the laughs, shared adventures and cocktails. There are far too many of you to name but you know who you are and that I love each of you.

My dear friend J.P. Ware, English teacher extraordinaire, was generous enough to be my first line editor. Not only is she a wordsmith in the most professional sense, her stories are woven into this book as well. My good friend Lucy Savage has devoted considerable time and creative energy to this project and, without her, this book would not be in print. My southern sister and soul mate, Linda Norton, served as my consultant on all details south of the Mason-Dixon Line as well as make-up and hairdos. I am blessed to have such good friends.

And then, of course, there is my family, who not only endured this project but, encouraged and supported me every step of the way. They served as my first proofreaders, made great suggestions and were very good natured about me sharing their stories with all of you. Most of all, they never wavered in their belief that I could do it. So, to my husband and sons – thank you, thank you, thank you. I love you very much.

Table of Contents

INTRODUCTION

I have to start out with an apology, which is never a good thing, but I feel as if I should get it out of the way immediately. If you bought this book because of the word "balancing" in the title, get your money back immediately. Implicit in the word balance are concepts such as equal weighting and control, implied in all of this is some sense of equilibrium. As near as I can tell, those are only scientific concepts that appear nowhere in the real world. So, as I said, I apologize if the title was misleading and, if you haven't wrinkled the binding of the book, by all means, return it. This is more of a survival guide.

This book is a reaction to all the people who have said to me, with a mixture of pity and contempt (and a great deal more contempt than pity), "Oh my my. How ever do you do it? You have so many balls in the air." Whenever anyone says something of that nature to me, I feel like turning to them, grabbing them by the throat and shrieking, in a most unladylike fashion, "Balls? Balls? No, these are not balls. Balls are either a part of the male private anatomy or little toys that, when you drop one, they bounce. What I am constantly tossing in the air are sticks of explosives, similar to the ones used to blast stumps out of the ground. If I drop one, the entire back of my house will get blown off. No, I can assure you, these are not balls, of either nature."

However, I never say anything to these fools because anyone who would make such an inane comment could not begin to comprehend such a response. In fact they would, more than likely, find it to be the rantings of a woman either on or slightly over the edge. Only a working mother would understand. Anyone else would probably think back to my Aunt Stella, the woman for whom the drug Prozac was invented, and conclude that such things just must run in my family.

It fairly staggers me to hear women who do not work outside the home and have relatively independent children complain about being exhausted. I want to make it clear here that I am not talking about the women who are involved with their children or the many who selflessly give their time and energy to charities and other worthy causes. Nor am I referring to those individuals who choose not to work for whatever personal reasons they may have. I would never presume to argue with or be judgmental of any personal choice. I have many close friends who fall into each category.

What I am talking about are the ones whose greatest problem is when their manicure gets canceled or the florist delivers the wrong color centerpiece yet, whenever you see them, they are exhausted and complaining about how overwhelmed they are. I have to ask, what is their problem? I realize I should probably be more open minded, but I just have to wonder. Did they have to park too far away from the door of the health club? Or are they just rung out from giving instructions to the housekeeper and the yardman? I don't get it. Even if they don't have household help, they can nap during the day. A nap that is a luxury I would trade a bag of gold for. Of course, if I had a bag of gold, I would probably be in the position where I could take a nap in the middle of the day, wouldn't I?

I can not imagine the possibility; peacefully sleeping when the stock market was open. If we could only impart that sense of the ultimate luxury to our pre-schoolers, it would forever end the "I-am-not-tired-and-don't-need-a-nap" argument. Good lord, can you imagine your boss coming up to you directly after lunch and saying, "Well okey-doke, time to get cozy on your sleeping mat, just relax for the hour if you don't think you can sleep."

And I am not talking here about the boss who suggests that the two of you get cozy together over at, say, the Four Seasons. No, I am talking about a pure nap, all alone, in the middle of the day. Hells bells, I would be sound asleep in a tetrasecond (which is VERY fast). The only problem would be waking me up.

I can give you a perfect example of just what I am railing about here. One of my son's friends showed our Christmas card to his mother, a woman whose biggest concern seems to be making sure her bag matches her shoes, and said to her, "Now this is a creative card. This is what Christmas cards are about." She looked at our card which, if I do say so myself, was quite clever and said with a harrumph, "Well some people have time for that sort of thing. I just don't have time to be creative." I guess all that shopping and personal training can really wear you out, not to mention the pressures of having to get your hair and make-up just right.

Just as Ptolemy and Galileo made observations about the universe and the forces that have an unseen, but surely felt effect upon our lives, I too have uncovered some of these governing forces. The reason Ptolemy and Galileo missed them is that they seem to effect only working mothers. For instance, why is it that every time there is a blizzard of more than eighteen inches of snow and I have a business obligation of such importance that my death would be the only acceptable excuse for a no-show; my husband just happens to be away on a golf trip?

I used to become furious and resentful and go through long periods of pouting upon his return each time this would happen. Now that I have realized that it is *The Golf Effect* on the weather patterns in the Northeast. I can accept it with grace. You see, once I realize something is being governed by a much higher power, I back away. Actually, in this case, I rummage through the junk drawer, trying to find the instruction manual detailing the operation of the snow blower and hope not to loose a limb in the process of liberating my car which has been thoroughly buried in the snow. Then, as I am driving away, hoping the kids don't burn the house down because, part of *The Golf Effect* is that school is always canceled and there is not a babysitter to be found, I wonder if I have thrown my back out trying to maneuver the snowblower. *The Golf Effect* does not just impact the weather in fact; it is such a powerful yet, until now, unexamined force that many pages in this book have been devoted to it.

Everyone is well acquainted with *The Dryer & Sock Force*. In fact, I am certain that I do not even have to detail it here, as it is universally acknowledged by every woman in the world who has ever done a load of laundry. But, what you may not have known is that it is one of the governing forces and absolutely impossible to overcome. Why, it would be easier to defy gravity.

If this is something which happens in your home, and I would be shocked to hear otherwise, after all, it is a force, you have to be creative. It cannot be stopped but it can be reckoned with. I'll share with you what I do. I only have one type of men's sock in the house. Everyone wears it and no one knows when one goes missing because all the other socks look exactly alike. I haven't ironed out all of the flaws in this remedy, such as the problem of playing tennis in high black executive hose, but as soon as I do, I will let you all know. After all, nothing is perfect and this is a book about survival, not perfection.

Another universal force over which we have no control is *The Sniffle Effect*. One of the things that makes it truly unique is, it has never affected a mother, but affects all husbands with equal devastation – howling paralysis. Not only for them, but if they are to be completely satisfied, their entire family's activities must come to a halt.

My husband's reaction, when anyone in the house gets sick is, "I hope I don't get it." He then proceeds to describe each illness he has contracted for the past ten years. This takes a long time because he considers himself to be sick each time he sneezes. He goes to bed and moans and expects to be waited on hand and foot. This makes it extremely difficult due to the fact that I have a very demanding full-time job. He accuses me of having terrible bed side manner and declares to anyone who will listen what a lousy doctor I would have been. Of course, I point out to him that had I indeed been a doctor, I would be taking care of sick people. My point escapes him as he immediately returns to detailing his symptoms and then making his dire self-diagnosis. Let me tell you, Web-MD has escalated this into a full blown nightmare. This is a man who is so concerned about the possibility of catching anything, he has absolutely no compunction about waking me up from a sound sleep and announcing, "You'd better wake up, someone is throwing up."

Someone? If I was not sprinting out of the room to find my sick child, I might ask him if he could be a little bit more specific with regard to whom, exactly, it might be, or if he actually thought it could possibly be a stranger who, when passing our house, suddenly felt nauseous and dashed in to barf in one of our bathrooms. When queried in this manner, he screws up his face and says, rather pathetically, "You know that I gag. . . . plus, they always want you." No one would wonder why – I don't come into their room with a germ mask on, telling them not to breathe in my direction.

To demonstrate how universal this is, all I have to say at work is, "My husband thinks he has a cold." Every woman within earshot says something to the effect of, "Oh, I feel so sorry for you." And then they begin to describe their husbands and how *The Sniffle Effect* takes control of their entire household. It is astounding to hear. Where do they learn this stuff? Is there some sort of class they attend, right before they get married?

And then come the 500 or so phone calls to work that start out with a grown man asking in a little baby voice, "Do you think you will be able to come home early?" You've got to wonder what he thinks would possibly be my motivation.

Then, "Do you think there are any special medicines that you should pick up for me on your way home – you are leaving early, aren't you?"

On call 250 I suggest to my secretary that we leave him on hold for a bit. She rolls her eyes and says, "You know he hates to be on hold. He'll just hang up and call right back." What she is really saying to me is, "He's your problem, not mine. You talk to him."

I begin to pull out my hair when I pick up the phone and hear him say, "What have you been thinking about fixing me for dinner?" Have I mentioned that it is only 10:30 AM? This makes for a very long day at work compounded by the fact I always end up staying late because I am forced to catch up on all I would have been doing when I was otherwise occupied fielding the avalanche of calls.

Could you possibly guess what my husband's favorite technological advancement of the 21st century is? I won't keep you hanging here. It's the gizmo that I bought when our youngest child was born, that allows me to take his (the baby's) temperature by just sticking it in his ear for two seconds and clicking. My husband was using it so often, I had to hide it and pretend I had no idea where it was. You only get so many of those plastic covers to protect the inner ear from germs; I had to take drastic action.

How are we to keep working under such an expectation? We have already exhausted all our colleagues' patience and understanding with the sicknesses that have swept through our homes, bringing one child down after another. How can we possibly expect their indulgence when it is our adult companion who is demanding 24-hour care, especially when anyone else would be at work when similarly afflicted? The correct answer is that we can't, however, that leaves us with the daily conundrum. Who should we piss off today? Talk

about "the things they don't teach you in business school."
Now that is a class that I could teach and it would be among
the most useful in the two years of study. I am not expecting
a call though because I realize these are all well kept secrets
that the business school industry does not want leaked.

As I was writing this book, I began to wonder if this was just
a North American problem or had it gone international. So,
I decided to do some international research and went to
Ireland. The fact that it was Ireland greatly facilitated the
research part because they speak English there and English
being my first, second and third language, made the
research much more productive. Although, there were times
when I was not entirely convinced it was, indeed, the same
language.

I first engaged a woman taxi driver about married life and
child rearing in Ireland. It wasn't long before she really got
going and told me she refers to her husband as "Mr. Myself
and Myself". We had a good laugh because I call my
husband, "Mr. It's All About Me". Then I asked her what it was
like when he was sick. I burst out laughing when she said,
"Oh dear, let me tell you something, that is nothing you want
to know anything about. The entire world must stop spinning
for the very fact that Himself has sneezed."

She seemed quite dismayed when I assured her it was an
international (come on, this is valid, two countries make it
international) problem. She was shaking her head as she
asked, "Followed them right across the Atlantic, did it?" She
really looked disappointed as she added, "How unfortunate
for you, I thought that was one thing that was left behind.
They're nothing but a bunch of babies in long pants, they

are. The good Lord certainly knew what he was doing when he left the birthin' to us, did he not?"

I agreed, of course, and then left her speechless when I described to her how, when I was in transition labor with my youngest child, my husband was talking to my doctor and he said, "I think I know how she is feeling. I just separated my shoulder playing hockey and that really hurt me a lot." My doctor, who is not only a woman with three children, but also a good friend of mine, looked at him and said, "Best that you remain silent through the rest of this."

When I went in for my post partum check-up she said, "Did he really say that, or did I just dream it?" Nope, not only did he say it, he was making his best effort to empathize. It's a good thing he's so cute.

I was having lunch with my good friend Ellen and we were talking about how smart we thought we were when we were growing up. Like me, she grew up watching *Ozzie and Harriet* and *Leave It to Beaver* with utter contempt for June and Harriet. We told ourselves that we would never live such a boring uncreative existence as those women. No way. We were going to go to college and graduate school and be independent women, in full control of our own destiny. Of this, we were certain.

We would also be the witty soul mate to our equally creative energetic spouse. We would decorate our homes and entertain our friends with gusto. And, of course, our children would be so appreciative that they had these superlative mothers, they would be perfect as well. Perhaps in gratitude, I don't really remember, but as I write this, I am scaring myself to think I could have been so far off base.

Ellen went to MIT and got a degree in math and then, because she may possibly be the smartest person I know, decided to go to their graduate school, the Sloan School of Management, to get a degree in finance. A truly staggering accomplishment, few will ever attempt, much less achieve.

While there, she met her wonderful husband, Patrick. He really is a great guy so the plan was looking really good. They got their MBA's and each began very successful careers. Everything was going great, according to plan, and their home was nothing like the Nelsons' or the Cleavers'. Nope, not one bit. Days would go by and the only communication they would share would be notes on the kitchen table and a phone call here or there. Two careers, two professionals. But, there was always time for the romantic dinner on Saturday or the weekend get-away. Roses arrived at the office and there was always time to run out and get just the perfect card for the perfect occasion. Just as I believed in the myth, Ellen felt that she could do it all – hell, she was.

And then came the babies – anticipated and welcomed, and very well loved. After all, babies were very much a part of "doing it all". Why even get married if you aren't going to have babies? What would you put on the perfect Christmas (or is that holiday?) card?

All of a sudden, as we were discussing at lunch, June and Harriet's gig didn't look too bad. They never had to throw sticks of explosives in the air - what the heck were we thinking? If you have asked yourself that question more than once, read on. You might find some helpful hints, hopefully have a laugh or two and know for sure, that you are not alone.

In The Beginning

"The hardest years in life are those
between ten and seventy."
-Helen Hayes (at age 73)

Of course, we didn't start out with careers, husbands, houses, children, dogs, and SUV's; it is a gradual process, some might say that it takes on a life of its own, much like the tides against the rocks. Eventually it will all become sand but no one will see it happen. Many of us had to battle each step of the way professionally and perhaps we took our eye off the ball a bit on the personal front. Some of us forgot to get married and have children or we didn't take the care in choosing a partner that we did a career. In our 20's it seemed as if there would always be time for everything, even a "do-over or two" but, of course, that was just an illusion. Perhaps delusion is a better word.

But for those of us that managed to progress down that path, it didn't happen all at once.

On September 9, 2001, *The New York Times* reported "This year the number of women entering law school is expected to exceed the number of men for the first time." That sure took a long time. All you have to do is to read an account of Ruth Bader Ginsburg's time at Harvard Law School. She was one of nine women in the class of 1959, in an era when there were many who did not support the concept of women in law. It has been reported that Dean Erwin Griswold actually asked the women of her (Ginsburg's) class what it felt like to occupy the places that could have gone to deserving men. You are probably gasping out loud, wondering how something so biased could possibly have been said, at such a renowned institute of higher learning. The thing that amazes me is that these women had the guts to put themselves into an environment where this sort of thinking was acceptable. We owe them all a great deal. Can you imagine how much smarter and more motivated than all of the men they had to be, just to be credible? The fact that one of these usurpers would go on to be the second woman and first Jew to be appointed to the Supreme Court is, no doubt, something that Dean Griswold would have found ludicrous, had it ever been suggested to him at the time.

When we were marching for equal pay for equal work, we were not taken seriously. "The Powers That Be" (I, incidentally, refer to this group as "The Fat White Boys") did not think that women earning sixty-seven cents for each dollar earned by a man, for the same work, was unfair. After all it was the women who had to take care of the home and bear the children - how could we be taken as seriously as a man with a career and no household responsibilities? Not to mention, what if one of their wives got the stupid idea of working - who would take care of them if their wife was at work? The thought was frightening enough for them to dismiss the concept in its entirety and throw up every road block they could think of. Their most effective weapon being to collectively never consider that a woman could be their professional peer. I wonder if there was a big meeting at Loch Ober one afternoon where they all agreed that this would be their best defense. Don't forget, it wasn't too many years earlier that women were publicly horse whipped for suggesting that they should be able to vote.

In one of my earlier professional positions, my boss was a graduate of one of the very prestigious law schools in the Boston area. He had often heard me say that I thought that our business, financial services, was behind the rest of the world in recognizing women as professionals.

With this in mind, one afternoon he gleefully brought his law school's alumni magazine in for me to read an article about women and the law. It seems it was the 35th (or some such number) anniversary of their first graduating class that included women. There were four or five, if I recall correctly. What I do remember, very clearly was the interview with one of these women.

She was asked what it was like, back then, trying to enter a very male dominated profession. She said that although she had graduated from this very prestigious law school, of international renown, she could not even get an interview at a law firm. Finally a godfather or family friend intervened and asked a good friend of his, a senior partner at one of the big Boston firms, to give her an interview.

She was not met by a lawyer but rather by a secretary, as they were then called. The secretary took her around the firm rather timidly, and didn't really have any information that this woman was interested in. When the tour was over, the senior partner, as a courtesy, had a "couple of minutes he could spare".

She described how intimidating it was to sit in this grand office and have this older man glaring at her. He fairly barked at her, "Do you have any questions?"

She surprised them both by saying, "Yes, yes I do have one."

He made no effort to conceal how annoyed he was when he asked her whatever might that be. She asked him if he could ever envision a woman partner in his firm. He was clearly undone by the very thought but, being a proper Boston lawyer, he gathered himself and gave her a very lawyerly response. "Yes, under certain circumstances, with certain conditions, I could envision that. Now do you have *any more* questions?" he asked her as he was rising to see her to his door.

She shocked herself by responding, "Yes. Under what circumstances and conditions would that be?"

He ended the "interview" by stating, without apology, "None whatsoever."

My boss was shocked when I told him that I did not think things had changed much since that time. It was just illegal to say it out loud but the collective pact had been made and it has taken a lot more than laws to break down the mindset.

My first child was born in 1980 - not so long ago on a time line but, I would argue, light years ago as far as the workplace goes. In 1982, when I applied for a professional position for which I was well qualified, I worked very hard not to disclose the fact that I had a two year old. I suspected then, and still believe, that I would not have been offered the position had that been known.

If he was sick and I had to stay home from work with him, I had to pretend I was sick because I would not have been taken seriously if I was missing work to care for my sick child. The unspoken sentiment would have been, "Why doesn't she just stay home like a good mother - like our wives do? Clearly she can't be committed to her career and her family." I still feel ashamed at how many times I bundled that little guy up and brought him to day care when he should have been at home, in his own bed, all because was afraid I would be "Mommy-Tracked".

For those of you not acquainted with that term, I am sorry to say it was (is?) a real term, often used with regard to a professional woman who had career aspirations and young children and, did not find them to be mutually exclusive. She might want to attend the second grade play or, yes, stay home with a sick child. Clearly this demonstrated a lack of commitment to the job and anyone with these priorities could not be taken seriously. I knew that I was smart and worked really hard, contributing as much to the organization as any of my peers, male or female. The fact that I was also the mother of a young child did not diminish that but, we were all forced to conceal how important our small children were to us. It was awful – you didn't even want to put a picture of them up in your office because it would remind someone that they existed and your loyalty would be questioned. Sometimes I would feel like a double agent – a job for which I learned I was not well suited.

The workplace has, in some ways, changed dramatically in the past 20+ years that I have been working in a professional capacity. As the blanket of "political correctness" falls over all of us some may welcome the arrival of a kinder and gentler office environment and some, no doubt, find it suffocating. I find myself somewhere in the middle.

As I have said, I believe that my industry, the "World of Wall Street," may have been one of the last holdouts. It was dominated by the Fat White Boys for so long and they so tenaciously hung on to all that was sacred to them, change came slowly.

The stories of the parties are the stuff of legends – traders jumping into the fish tanks at the Boston Aquarium (a very expensive party as all of the fish had to be taken out and the tanks had to be drained and cleaned), conga lines at the Waldorf, belly shots at fancy Boston restaurants, naked limbo contests, with everyone, always, drunker n'Ole Cooter Brown – as an old boyfriend of mine used to say.

I am going to digress here for a moment with a discussion topic: Can someone in the north actually get "drunker n' Ole Cooter Brown" or do you have to be south of the Mason-Dixon Line?

My response: You can immediately envision the level of inebriation being described. No one would make the mistake of thinking it was just a little buzz, even if they had never met anyone named Cooter, much less the actual ole Cooter Brown himself (I am assuming that Cooter would be a male.) Therefore, I think I'm alright here, this is not a regional condition of being over-served, but rather something anyone could immediately envision. You can let me know what you think.

Back to the workplace of old. There was no such thing as sensitivity training, there were pictures of naked women hanging in trading rooms and, at some firms, sexual harassment was a corporate sport. A very large brokerage firm was actually sued for having among other things, (I am not joking) a "Boom-Boom Room." This is not the stuff of rumors; it has been well documented in the press. The everyday language was extremely creative and could make a steel worker take a deep breath.

As Gerald Ford said, "The pendulum has come full circle." We now have mandatory workshops and continuing education classes that focus on sexual harassment (also mandatory for all of us on Wall Street) and there is a new atmosphere of restraint and decorum.

That is, unless you happen to be the President of the United States. I think Bill Clinton personally set women in the workplace back at least ten years. I remember the chant, "The dress is a mess, he must confess."

All of a sudden, everyone was talking about blow jobs again. Who could blame them? They had been dying to resurrect their favorite topic and here was the perfect opportunity. It was, for the first time in history, an international discussion point.

You do have to ask yourself what was that child thinking, hanging onto that dress in it's, shall we say, "violated state"? This would not be something you would save to show your children. Perhaps the answer is in the question – she was just a child but, whatever was *he* thinking? I guess if Ken Star couldn't find out after spending all of that money, the rest of us will never know. I just wish he hadn't gone on television shaking his finger at all of us as if we were idiots.

One thing I have noticed as we are spreading all of this "awareness" around is that some of the youngins can take it a little too far. There is nothing wrong with getting coffee for someone, if it helps things move along. We should all remember that we have the same objective, which is to provide our clients with the best products and service possible. Whenever that happens, we all benefit.

I am a Managing Director of the firm but, like everyone else, I do my own typing, make my own copies and do whatever it takes, to get the job done, as time permits. If I ever ask anyone to do something like that for me it is because I don't have the time to do it myself.

I think back to the time, at a previous firm, when I was meeting with clients in my office and we needed copies of some of the material we were discussing. I came out of my office and asked a temporary employee, who was filling in for my assistant, to make me some copies. She looked up at me and, in a very haughty tone, informed me that she had gone to college and the copier was down the hall.

You know the silence that sets in, directly after all activity ceases and everyone's attention is directed at the one place where they feel something really good or really bad is about to happen? Well, that's what occurred and although I was momentarily stunned, as was everyone else in the immediate area, I thanked her for the information and asked her to make the copies on her way out. I am sure she still thinks I am one of the worst people alive but, perhaps now, she gets it. I hope so for her sake or she will find herself with a long string of very brief jobs.

My point here is: be smart – understand your corporate culture. Don't allow someone to treat you like a serf but, on the other hand, look around, pitch in – don't be afraid to roll up your sleeves if you see something that needs to be done. We all need to pay our dues – you just don't have to do it in a manner anymore that makes you feel uncomfortable, threatened, compromised or unsafe. That is a very good thing and a hard fought victory. Understand it for what it is and don't use it as an excuse to be a slacker.

It has been interesting to watch Jane Swift, the acting governor of Massachusetts. She gave birth to twin girls while in office and it was absolutely amazing to watch her political adversaries use her pregnancy and her daughters' birth as at opportunity to take pot shots at her. When it backfired completely, as the public, Democrats and Republicans alike were outraged, theses hacks all ran for cover. It was really pathetic.

Her doctors told her that she needed bed rest, a situation that many women carrying twins find themselves in. She followed their instructions of course and continued to run the State, from her hospital bed. She chaired a meeting, which she attended by conference call. They tried to say that she didn't have the authority over the phone that she would have had, had she been there in person and declared the proceedings invalid. Wouldn't you love to talk to the brain trust that thought that one up?

As Daniel Golden pointed out in *The Wall Street Journal*, the governor of Rhode Island had recently taken five weeks off following surgery for prostrate cancer. As he stated, "No clamor was heard for an interim replacement, not even from the Democratic lieutenant governor, who would have gotten the job." Of course, the governor of Rhode Island is a man and Governor Swift is a woman. Golden went on to write, "To many women juggling demands of career and maternity, that gender difference helps to explain why Governor Swift is under increasing pressure from some Democrats to step down until she can resume her duties full-time." So much for progress.

Governor Swift has also created some controversy by talking about establishing a breast feeding room in the Massachusetts State House. I think this is a great idea. Many women, who return to work after giving birth, still want to be able to provide their babies the advantages of their breast milk. A woman that I work with has recently returned to work after giving birth to her first child. Fortunately for her, she lives close enough to our office to allow her to go home at lunch, schedule permitting. However, there are days when she can not get away; she is an attorney and has a very hectic and demanding schedule. When that happens, she has her nanny bring the baby into the office or she uses a breast pump to keep her milk flow steady. She found that she had to have a lock put on her office door because it wasn't enough to merely shut the door. Our mostly male colleagues would get quite a surprise as they rushed in, eager for a legal opinion and there she was, with her boob attached to a breast pump. It has been the cause of more than one to forget their urgent question.

When my youngest son was born in 1988, things were a bit different. I had prepared my presentation for the quarterly board meeting, anticipating that I would not be there to present. I gave it to my boss and reviewed it with him in detail, asking him to present in my absence. The day before the board meeting, he called me in a panic. He did not understand the information and couldn't I possibly make the presentation. I had to go and do it.

I told him that I had a six day old baby who couldn't be away from me for more than two hours. Without even thinking of the implication of my statement he just said, "Bring him with you."

Not being smart enough to say, "Are you kidding me?", I bundled up my new baby (it was in December) and off we went to the board meeting. I set him down, right in the middle of the huge mahogany table, surrounding him with gray hair and Brooks Brothers suits. He appeared nonplussed, sleeping through most of my presentation.

Displaying great sensitivity, they put me first on the agenda. I opened the meeting, moving through my material as quickly as possible and was actually thinking that I might make it through without any sort of a disaster. Things were fine for the first hour or so, and then I could feel my milk starting to come in. When you have just given birth, this is a sensation that can not be described to anyone who has not experienced it. Suffice it to say, I could feel my boobs getting bigger and bigger by the second. As I desperately tried to wrap up my presentation, the questions were flying and it became painfully apparent (literally) to me that this story was not going to have a happy ending. I thought both of my boobs were going to explode right off my body, drenching all of them sitting around the table with breast milk. It would have finished two or three of them off right there. Their hearts could have never withstood such an event, and would have exploded out of their chests, right beside my boobs. Good Lord, that visual is enough to make me go have a glass of wine.

Then, I started leaking – not just little drops – more like water rushing through a burst dam. Then, my son started to make those little baby squeaks – perhaps he could smell his lunch, just bringing the milk in faster.

Finally, I couldn't stand it any longer and answered a

question by saying, "I would be happy to answer that but, I have to feed my son." There was some nodding for a second or two until the collective realization set in that there was not a bottle in sight. This caused a stampede of gray suits and wing tips, charging through the board room doors more rapidly than if I had yelled, "Fire!" In very short order, my son and I had the board room to ourselves.

He enjoyed his lunch, quite unbothered by all that had transpired. I had to throw that suit away as my milk had soaked all the way down to the skirt and the dry cleaners could never get it all out. So, you can see why I applaud Governor Swift's breast feeding room. That is progress and, I have to remind myself how far things have come. It's easy to get upset at the things that haven't changed but I try to never lose sight of how things were "in the beginning".

Now, thanks to a combination of technology and what I shall call "workplace awareness" we have the flexibility to, on occasion, work from home, which turns out to be a good deal for everyone. There is little that makes me angrier than when I see someone (yes, both men and woman) taking advantages of this flexibility. To do so, sets us all back because, there are still many "non-believers" out there, anxious to return things to the "good old days". It's a privilege, a benefit, not an entitlement and should be used with care otherwise, we all get hurt.

I still shudder when I think of the time when my oldest child was about three and I was trying to work from home, without anyone knowing – my friends and I referred to that as "under the cover of darkness". I was on the telephone with a client, having a very serious conversation when, unbeknownst to me, my son had woken from his nap and hopped out of his bed. He heard me talking on the telephone and assumed it was my father to whom I was speaking. He made that assumption because my father was the only person he ever talked to on the phone therefore, who else could it be?

My blood ran cold as I heard the upstairs extension being picked up - I had no idea how to stave off this disaster. The phone banged around a bit and then I heard him say, in his little three year old voice, "Hi Da, you take me fishing? I'm sick today - I fro up."

Well, I was about to throw up - I saw my all too brief career spin past my eyes and felt completely helpless. I was certain my client would never take me seriously again and was nearly in tears, desperately trying to think of some sort of a plausible explanation. Nothing was coming, just that sick ache you get in your stomach when everything is going wrong. It's probably the way someone standing in front of a firing squad feels.

My client, a rather stern 60-ish gentleman said, in his very gruff voice, "What was THAT?" I told him rather meekly that it was my son and he was too sick to go to daycare so, I was trying to work from home. It would have been just as easy to have told him that I had been arrested for selling military secrets to the Soviets (there was still a Soviet Union at that that time).

There was a long pause (when your life is passing before your eyes it seems as if it is taking a long time) and he said, "My daughters all work and they have small children. I don't know how you girls do it. Don't worry, your secret is safe with me.

Now go take care of your son and call me when you get back into work."

The first of many bullets dodged.

I look back on those early years of his with so much guilt. Even though he has grown into a sweet, charming, affable, well balanced man, with whom I have always had a wonderful relationship, I am horrified by the memories of how many frantic mornings I raced with him from the house, threw him into his babyseat (luckily, they weren't nearly as complicated then as now), tossed him a doughnut and a juice box, jammed my car into reverse and roared out of the driveway. What a peaceful image. It is a testimony to DNA only that he is so laid back. When I ask him about those days, with tears in my eyes, he just laughs and says, "It was fine Mum, don't worry about it."

I vowed back then, that when (and it was never "if" but always "when" – the misplaced confidence of youth) I was the boss, my expectations would accommodate people's lives, to include their children. I sincerely hope that this is something I have accomplished professionally.

The Boston Globe interviewed Shirley M. Tilghman, Princeton's first female president in their 255 year history. This appeared on July 10, 2001, in the Living/Arts section and I read the interview with great interest, not because I have any opinion with regard to whether or not Princeton should have a female president but rather because of the quote that was bolded above President Tilghman's photograph. She was quoted as saying, "When I was at work, I thought about work. I did not think about the children. I did not feel guilty. When I left, I put on the Mom switch."

I was blown away by this statement. I wrote her a letter and asked her if she felt that statement had been taken out of context or if it accurately reflects the way she feels. I asked her, in my letter, if she was able not to think about her children when they were sick or if they had a big test. How about if they had tryouts or got cut from a team or had a fight with one of their best friends? On the days of a big game or when anything at all important to them is happening? I have not yet heard back from her and don't really expect to, after all, she is pretty busy, being the first woman president of Princeton and all.

Another thing she was quoted saying in this article was that she thinks Princeton should "begin to attract people with green hair". I'll bet that made a lot of Princeton alumni pretty happy. Perhaps, because it was in the Living/Arts section, they'll miss it. But, if I was willing to guess, I would say that she would have received more mail about the green hair than about the Mom switch. I wonder where you get one of those switches; perhaps, at Princeton.

I showed this article to a couple of my friends, just to see if their reaction was similar to mine. Not surprisingly, it was. The conversation then moved on to green hair at Princeton. I asked if they could ever imagine anyone at Princeton with green hair and we were having a lively discussion about this until my friend Sally pointed out that she didn't know anyone who went to Princeton who had any hair at all so, it became a moot subject.

I mention this not to single out President Tilghman. I think that it is really great that she has reached such a lofty level of professional accomplishment. I also think it's great that she is willing to be a "ground breaker" at Princeton. The only other Ivy League college with a woman president is the University of Pennsylvania. Judith Rodin has been their president for seven years. Brown University will have Ruth Simmons as their president, beginning in November 2001. I think this is really a big deal and another great step forward for all of us, especially those being educated.

I don't need to mention that President Tilghman is much smarter than I (an understatement, by all accounts, she is brilliant), better educated and has reached a much higher level professionally. However, I really wish that she believed she could have done all of it – because I am certain that she could have – without her Mom Switch.

Let's get back to my initial thought – we didn't start out with everything: careers, spouses, children, houses, dogs, SUV's, but rather acquired them gradually, over a period of time. But once begun, I would argue that the Law of Inertia takes over. Everyone understands half of this Newtonian Law: an object at rest remains at rest. You often hear people use inertia as an explanation of why something stopped and never started again. But, what I find is that many people don't know that is only half of the Law. The second part says that "An object in motion tends to remain in motion." That's what happened to a lot of us. We set ourselves in motion and never stopped. Do you think it might be Newton's fault?

One of the things I wanted to explore when I was in Ireland was if this was something that was limited to the United States or if it was an international happening. I went to a library to see if I could find any documentation on this one way or the other. While flipping through many magazines, I came across the October 2001 issue of *SHE Magazine* which bills itself "a magazine for busy modern women". In that issue I found an article talking about a poll conducted by Clinique, the cosmetics firm called, *"Evolution Clinique: A Vision of Women in 2020".*

It seems they polled 800 women across the UK for this project where they report: "The notion of having it all (which suggests that combining a career, home and relationship is effortless) has been replaced by the more realistic idea of doing it all (combining career, home & relationship is hard work, although undoubtedly rewarding)." And this wasn't even translated from another language.

The article also quoted Dr. Linda Austin, professor of psychiatry at the Medical University of South Carolina who said, "While women are grabbing the ever-increasing new opportunities at work, they're finding it difficult to let go of traditional responsibilities at home."

Is Dr. Austin suggesting that after being out of the house for twelve to fourteen hours, between their commute and actual work time, women are reluctant to have someone else clean their bathroom? I have yet to meet these women, although that is not to say they don't exist somewhere.

This article called the work/life balance, "the new dilemma". Perhaps it is new in the UK but all they have to do is look across the ocean and they will see plenty of us who have been fighting the battle for decades. If this wasn't enough to make me realize that the magazine's target audience was an age group much younger than mine, the final realization came when I saw who these 800 women voted the "most modern woman in the public eye". Madonna.

Madonna is probably a lovely woman and a terrific mother. After all, she and Rosie are good buddies but give me a break. Can you see Madonna in a car pool line? Or making the snack to bring to pre-school? If this is what they are aspiring to, I think they will be sorely disappointed. Or perhaps, as they move forward, they will modify their expectations.

But, one thing we do know is they will move forward, whether as a result of a Newtonian force or something else, because once we are in motion, we do tend to remain in motion.

Nowadays there is no particular order in which these things must occur. In the days of the Cleavers and Nelsons it was pretty clear cut, especially for the woman. She found a man and got married. After the wedding, they bought a house and a bunch of matching appliances and then had their babies. If they were lucky, perhaps they bought a second car after the children were born, perhaps not. If there was one car, it was really big and might have been a beach wagon, with the fake wood on the sides. I loved those. We never had one when I was growing up and I always thought that once I was a mom, it would be the first thing I would buy. I also used to eat marshmallow fluff right out of that white plastic container it came it.

Now these things can happen in any order you choose, as many times as you choose. But, for the purposes of this book, let's roughly use the career-partner-house-children timeline. Of course, you could have a house and children when you meet your partner – he/she could have the same. You may or may not have done it all before. But, I am writing a survival guide here, not an encyclopedia so, we are going to make certain simplifying assumptions.

I guess the first decision we must make is "when" to start the process, assuming that we are working already, when is the best time to get married? One of the things that has always perplexed me is that, if you read any of those studies, everyone seems to agree that married men live longer and are happier than single men however, single women live longer than married women. Yet, everyone also seems to think that women are dying to get married – hey, maybe that's it. It's a death wish. No, I'm just kidding. All parties seem to think that men avoid marriage vigorously, preferring to have their fingernails ripped off but it is the answer to all women's prayers. I would like to find the source of this misinformation. I would surely have a few things to say to him. And yes, I am sure it is a man.

Anyway, back to the "right time". I can answer that one. There is no "right time". If you find the right person, just do it. The rest of the stuff will sort itself out. There are several pages further on in this book that will assist you in determining if you have indeed found the "right" person. This can be deceiving so, be careful, just sort of tip toe along. It is much easier to move forward slowly than to try to back track. Once you have given up some ground, it becomes the sovereign state of the givee and very tough to reclaim.

Once the result of the 2000 census was published, thousands of articles popped up telling us all about ourselves as a nation and how we have changed demographically in the past decade. I think a lot about this sort of thing and found all of this data mining fascinating, especially the family stuff. People on each side of the political spectrum picked out the data that supported their political agenda and used it to advance their cause(s). That is one of the beautiful things about statistics.

Anyway, I had piles and piles of newspapers and magazines all around the house with little "stickies" marking the articles I wanted to save. The entire house became an obstacle course, where one had to maneuver around my piles to get from one room to another. My husband (sometimes called Captain Tidy) finally threatened to call the fire department and have the house declared a fire hazard. I had to pick and choose what I kept. I hope he never looks under our bed.

On July 17, 2001, in the Sunday Styles section *The New York Times* published a piece called "Life With Father Isn't What It Used to Be", where they profiled a single dad, an unwed dad and a nuclear dad. Joe Queenan, whom I really enjoy reading, wrote the profile about himself, the nuclear dad. It was very funny. He began by mentioning that much of the nation was shocked and disappointed to learn, as a result of the recent census, that "Nuclear Families" now make up less than one quarter of the households in America. But not Joe, he was not the least bit surprised. He went on to say, "Viewing marriage as a sort of emotional endurance test, and parenthood as a brutally demanding, financially ruinous, yet emotionally fulfilling decathlon, I am proud to say that my wife, my 17 year old daughter, my 14 year old son and myself have been able to stay the course and remain "nuclear" in the truest sense of the word. Even though I strongly suspect that they all secretly hate me."

He went on to state that in no way did he feel any moral superiority to those families that, for whatever reasons, have opted out of the "Nuclear Model". He wrote, "In many cases, nuclear families have retained their monadic status simply because their children refuse to leave or because the children are not strong enough to force one or more parents to clear out." He then described what he refered to as the "dysfunctionally nuclear family": "For example, in households where one or more of the parents actively despise their children or where the children loathe one or both parents, or where everyone dislikes a grandparent who stubbornly refuses to check into an assisted-care facility, one witnesses a dynamic best described as the King Lear syndrome. . . . .In households where mutual apathy runs rampant, one comes face to face with a social unit best listed under the rubric thermonuclear family." I found this to be hilariously accurate and thank him for sharing these observations with all of us.

I include this not to discourage you from marriage but only to remind you, things are often not what they first appear to be. And, as Maisey, my Irish grandmother who was the major source of any wisdom imparted to me in my youth, often said, "Oh Child, let me tell you, there are many things worse than not being married." So, just be careful what you wish for and keep your eyes wide open at all times.

If you do go forward and decide to marry you will be faced with the dilemma that women have been faced with for the past 20 or 30 years which is, do you take his name? The chairman of one of the companies for which I worked (who has four daughters) could never get past any woman not taking her husband's name. He was genuinely personally outraged and would ask ridiculous things such as, "What happens when you check into a hotel together?" We would attempt to explain to him that it's only in some Middle Eastern countries where a woman with a different name would be considered a prostitute and not allowed to check in with her husband. He didn't get it though. He also thought that they would be a poor credit risk and that no one should grant them a mortgage, regardless of how much money they made or had. Scary.

By the way, I have no advice one way or the other on that subject, it is truly what you and your husband work out but I will suggest you go about it differently that my husband and I did. When we were applying for our marriage license, the city clerk said to me, "Will you be changing your name?" Much to my surprise, as I was saying, "No." my soon-to-be-husband was saying, "Yes."

The city clerk made no attempt to hide her disdain as she said, "Isn't this something you two should have discussed before now?" It is difficult to argue with her point.

The next "when" is when is the right time to have children – buying a house is strictly a financial decision, there isn't really a "when" involved other than "when" you have the money. I can tell you right now, there is no right time, other than when you and your partner feel that it's right for you. Just go for it.

Last summer I hired a wonderful young woman who is married to a great guy and I knew they did not have any children. She was in her late 20's, early 30's, had just bought a very nice new house and was very happily married. I figured that a family was part of the near term plan and was stunned when she came to me in tears, about six months after she started working for me, to tell me she was pregnant. Stunned, not because she was pregnant, hell, I had figured that was coming; stunned because she thought I would be upset. I asked her why she was crying and she said she was afraid I would think it was "too soon". I told her she was crazy, that you should never plan your life around your job, if at all possible. I really mean that and am delighted to report she has a lovely new son and will be coming back to work very soon.

But, I am jumping ahead here, let's get you married first. This is big and deserves a chapter or two all to itself.

Choose Wisely

"You see a lot of smart guys with dumb women, but you hardly ever see a smart woman with a dumb guy."

-Erica Jong

There are many reasons to get married - some certainly more practical than others. For instance, you can get married for financial stability. There are worse reasons. Not many but, I digress. However, if you do choose that route, bear in mind Maisey's (my previously introduced Irish grandmother) caution. I can still hear her saying, in that wonderful brogue that she never surrendered, even after 50 years in this country, "Oh Child, doone ya know, that when you marry for money, you 'arn it every day."

But, that's not to say it's always a bad idea, just almost always. I guess it is really all a matter of expectations. A friend of mine, who is "earning her money every day", had me to her home for lunch. Of course, she was a bit put out it had to be on the weekend because I work, but being the good friend that she is, she made allowances. We were sitting in her grand kitchen overlooking the harbor, discussing this very topic when she turned to me and said rather matter-of-factly, "Well Sweetie, I do realize that money can not buy you happiness but, it sure as shit can take the sting out of being miserable." She nearly blinded me as the sun reflected off her various jewels, as she was waving her hand around. Who could argue with that? Again, it's all in managing your expectations.

When I tell the young women I work with that they should not even think about getting married until they have had at least one knock-down-drag-out-full-blown-donnybrook with their man, I get a mixed response. I explain to them patiently that there is a lot to be learned about someone when the gloves come off and the fur flies. For instance, you learn, in no uncertain terms, exactly what he thinks about your mother, your sister and your best friend. If his opinions extend to how your derrière looks in blue jeans, you might want to rethink things.

The women who laugh and say, "Oh yeah, no kidding" and begin to detail one of their own battles are not the ones I worry about. It's the ones who look at me, with pity in their eyes and say, "Oh no, that is foolish. Charles would never raise his voice to me... And me, well, I could never be mad at him, he is just too dear......" that I worry about. Because, as sure as you and I are sitting here, the day will come when Charles will raise his voice and then some and she will be so unprepared, so blown away, that she may never recover.

I did my duty as the elder, I warned her. If she doesn't listen, if she believes that she is the exception to the rule well, it's just not my fault. One thing I have come to learn in life is that whenever you think you, your partner, or one or your children are the exception to the rule, there is an extremely high probability that you are mistaken. It is a very precarious state of mind to be in.

I do not want to give the impression that I am dumping on the youngins because that would not be at all accurate. I think this younger generation of women is approaching the entire concept of "sharing household duties" in a much smarter way than we did. We felt we could do it all. But I suppose if I were to be completely honest, I can't pretend that I do it all. In my household, we have a clear division of labor. My husband takes the trash out on Mondays and operates his snowblower, in the unlikely event he is home when we have a blizzard. I do everything else, in addition to having a full-time job which is, incidentally, his excuse why he shouldn't have to do more.

There is an explanation for this completely illogical situation, sort of. My friend, Lucy has a theory that there must have been something in the baby formula (no, our mothers did not breast feed, it was too sexual) in the years from 1945 - 1960. It could have had something to do with WWII, she hasn't worked that part of the theory out but, whatever it was, she believes and I concur, that little baby girls born in that time period grew into women suffering under the delusion that not only could we do it all, but that we wanted to. That is the "Wonder-Woman Complex", or "WWC", which doesn't qualify as a universal force due to the fact it only effected babies born for a ten to fifteen year period. Perhaps this is an example of nature correcting herself once she realized the damage she had done. It also does not affect all of the baby girls born in that time period. There is a most definite northern skew to the dispersion but not enough to call it a regional thing. It was, most surely, a national phenomena, albeit, short lived.

The men did not support us in our efforts, nor did they welcome us when we arrived, dressed for battle, or business, as the case may be. They were very clear they did not want us in their business schools, their private dining rooms or on their golf courses. They did not want birth control easily accessible (that's one way to keep us home) and they did not ever want to consider the possibility of having a woman for a colleague, much less a boss.

But on we came. We fought to get into their business schools, we sued for membership in their all men's clubs and restaurants and took up golf with a vengeance. Well, some of us took up golf, the rest of us were not willing to go that far. I mean, we do have standards. As Bette Midler says, "They may be low, but we do have standards."

We quickly saw the result of our efforts. Women now have nearly as many heart attacks and strokes as men, their ulcers are bleeding and Congress refuses to do away with the "marriage-penalty" tax. You really have to ask yourself, whose idea this was anyway? Does any of this remind you of Tom Sawyer getting his fence painted?

But, back to the youngins. They have certainly figured out something that we have missed and, if I am forced to admit it, I think I am a bit envious. I love to watch them driving around town. They are quite easy to spot and can be found in any suburban town around the country, as they all drive those enormous, gas guzzling, four wheel drive vehicles, with those Thule things on top, holding all types of expensive completely up to date athletic equipment and little hockey players popping out of all the doors and windows. They have important meetings organizing car pools and setting up tennis matches, always conducted over lunch, often with Margaritas. They work out extensively and do not have one ounce of body fat on them (can you just hear my jealousy?) and despite giving birth to all of those little hockey players and a few ballerinas, they still look great in a bikini. (You should hear me trying to rationalize why I don't to my husband. It's pitiful.) They carry their leather bound appointment books and cell phones with them at all times, being prepared as they are, for an unexpected change in the day's events. I think they have their cell phones so they can call their husbands to remind them to make more money. Oh, and did I mention? They are always out of breath, and in an enormous rush to get somewhere. Otherwise, they would love to stop and chat with you. Alice's White Rabbit comes to mind.

One night when dining out, my husband, one son and I sat next to a table of five of them. It was impossible not to overhear their conversation which centered around the division of labor within their households. As near as I could tell, it was just about 50/50. I would have stood up and cheered, had I not realized that not one of them held down a job outside their home. One was recounting a harrowing business trip her husband has just taken. It had taken him about fifteen hours to get home from a business meeting half way across the country. As she described him dragging into the house, starved and exhausted, I was imaging Dr. Zhivago after he crawled across Siberia. One of the other women looked at her and said, "Oh that sounds just awful. Poor Henry. But, he still completed his share of home responsibilities, didn't he?" To which this man's wife said, with some surprise the question had even been asked, "Well yes, of course." I thought I was going to have to call 911 for my husband as his face was so purple, I thought he was stroking out on me. At least I don't have to worry about any of them reading this book.

As I was saying, before I got all carried away, thinking about the youngins, there are lots of reasons to get married, some better than others. We touched briefly on "financial stability". This can be really tricky for all of the obvious reasons, the most obvious reason being, he might lose all of his money, and then, where would you be? Or, an equally chilling possibility is that he might not let you spend any of it, believing that it is his alone to dole out. I get woozy just thinking about having to ask for money any time I wanted to make a purchase other than groceries. Money places a very powerful, though unseen, dynamic into a relationship.

This is one of the most compelling reasons why many of my friends choose to work outside the home, despite having ample financial resources, generated by their husbands. When you make these choices, many men don't like it. They say things to your husband like, "What do you have her working for, when she could be home, focusing exclusively on you and all of your desires, no matter how trivial?"

Although I know that exclusive focus would have enormous appeal to my husband, I still like to think that when he is asked this sort of question, he rides to my rescue like a gallant knight, proclaiming that I am a well educated woman, schooled in the financial markets and desirous of never having to depend on anyone. Unfortunately, history would indicate that he merely shrugs and says something like, "Why don't you try telling her not to do something? See how far it gets you."

There are times that my husband just about jumps for joy about me being a working woman, such as whenever a bill is presented and we both are present. He turns to me and says, "Oh gee, I don't have any money, I forgot to go to the bank." That ploy was working quite well until one evening, our youngest son was with us and, when my husband announced that he had not gone to the bank, our son said, "Oh yes you did Daddy. You have two hundred dollars." He then, bless his little heart, went over and pulled the money out of the pocket where he had observed his father stash it. I hope you can appreciate just how angry I was, not for the fact that he paid for dinner that evening, but for all of the previous dinner checks he had weaseled out of.

Now that we have exposed a few weaknesses in "financial stability" motivation as a reason to get married, let's discuss some of the other motivations. Because there are so many varying themes on this topic, I will try to stick with those most familiar to all of us. (In most cases, by the universe of "all of us", I am referring to my very good friends and myself. Believe it or not, this is actually, what I would believe to be a statistically viable universe.) There are some that we can eliminate right away, that are so foolish they do not even warrant discussion. They are, in no particular order:

- Because I Was Tired of Being Alone
- Because He Was So Good Looking
- Because It Seemed Like the Right Time
- Because All of My Friends Were Getting Married
- Because My Parents Loved Him
- Because My Parents Hated Him
- Because I Wanted to Have a Baby
- Because I Thought He Would Stop Drinking, Drugging, Womanizing (choose one or more)
  and this, being my particular all time favorite
  bad reasons:
- **Because He Asked Me To.**

This is by no means an exhaustive list.

Should you ever hear one of your dear friends utter any of these excuses, it is your duty to point out to them the ridiculousness of what they have just told you. This is one of the few times in life where a slap in the face might be warranted, if you have tried everything else. Believe me, she will forgive the slap and be eternally grateful for the life you have spared her from.

We have been contemplating reasons to get married, of which, everyone seems to agree at least in theory, there are many. Unfortunately, the reasons the majority of us choose to get married are fleeting and, in most cases, involve the very slippery concept of love.

A conundrum which I have often pondered is that, we all want to be with someone who is dynamic, thus by definition, evolving, changing, as it were. I mean who would want to be with someone who didn't come up with any new material for forty years?

And, the reasons he has chosen you are similar - your dynamic personality, your joie de vivre, your ability to continually surprise and delight him. So far, I'll bet your thinking, "So, what's wrong with that?" Here comes the conundrum. What are the chances that you two dynamic people are going to change in any way that is compatible? Catch my drift? So, at first it appears you have only two choices: end up with someone who is telling the same jokes forty years down the road or have a short, but delightfully exciting, romance. If I were to study the divorce rates in this country, I might be forced to conclude that number two is the more popular option. But, do not despair. I have given a great deal of thought to this, studied many pairs of people and lord knows, read many, many books on the topic and have concluded that the picture is not as bleak as I have painted. It's all a manner of managing your expectations.

I recognize that this is not a simple task but, the reason I have devoted so much time and energy to this analysis is not because I am afraid of divorce. No, not at all. In fact, in many instances it is the only acceptable solution to an untenable situation. What I am afraid of is having us go to all the trouble, financial and otherwise, not to mention the time it takes, to get ourselves divorced and then, what do we do? Well, you know precisely what it is we do. We go out and find ourselves another one, who may not have the exact same flaws but, we could probably switch 'em in the dark and never know.

Having observed the musical chairs of romance, I have often made this observation, without the scientific documentation to back it up. Well, that was before the Internet. I now have my documentation, which supports what we have all known, all along. Please flip to the Appendix and read the examples of gender differences, clearly laid out there, as fine as any Nobel thesis. These fine pieces have been sent to me via the Internet, by many different people, who have just forwarded them along. Unfortunately, I can not credit the authors because I do not know who they are. But, if any of you happen to be reading this book, thank you very much for providing me the supporting evidence that I have always intuitively known existed. I can not tell you how very grateful I am.

Whenever I show any of these to a woman, she carefully reads through the parts about the female, nodding and in full agreement the entire time, saying things such as, "Well, of course. What would you expect?" Then she gets to the part about the guys and she begins to frown, shake her head slightly and say things like, "Oh Lord, I thought my man was the only one who did THAT. Ohmagawd, you mean to tell me THEY ALL think that is funny?" I think you get the picture and, I am willing to guess you may have said some of the very same things as you were reading through them. I have always suspected this but, to see the empirical evidence so clearly laid out is, in an odd way, gratifying.

Then you show them to a man who quickly scans the first line or two about women, makes some dismissive animal like sound, and moves directly to the part about the men. He then breaks into hilarious laughter, reading the more disgusting things out loud, and finding not the tiniest thing wrong with these descriptions of male behavior.

There is one of these, entitled, "The Perfect Day", however it is far too offensive to be included in this book. It does sum things up, bringing it right down to brass tacks, as it were. The woman's perfect day involves a lot of pampering, bathing, lunching and cuddling. The man's day involves a great deal of bodily functions, sex with teenage nymphomaniacs, lots of red meat, brandy, cigars and, of course, golf at Augusta, no less. Every single man I have ever shown this to is virtually weeping at the conclusion, so jealous is he that he has never spent such a day. Each woman I have shown it to nods her head with disgust and acknowledges that after such a day her husband could die a happy man. How do we ever come together? Sex is a very powerful force.

You are wondering what my point is? I think it should be obvious. They are all nearly the same. They may look a little different, some are taller than others, some have more hair but, that could be a temporary thing. Some have more money than others but, we have already covered that. To recap, it's best to make or inherit your own.

What I am exposing is a very well kept secret, kept in large part by the American Bar Association. That is, you can go to all the trouble and expense of changing out your man and the chances are pretty high that you end up with another one who has all the same things that annoyed you about the first one. They may not be the exact same ones but they will be so similar, it won't make a bit of difference. You may have a short grace period before they emerge, if you are lucky.

All is not lost. It is up to us to recognize what we have in front of us and make it into something that works for us. How do we accomplish this? We manage our expectations. We go into this with our eyes wide open, understanding that there are certain things that you will get, no matter what package you choose. For instance, there is not a straight man in America who can let anyone else hold the clicker in his house. My husband has stooped so low as to hide it, even if he wasn't watching television. Fortunately he is not too creative in his hiding places and the children always uncover them in short order, averting an unpleasant scene. I have never met an American man who does not thoroughly enjoy passing gas. I am sorry girls, this is a fact. Some of them hide it for a time but once they, shall we say, let it rip, you might as well give up the ghost. After that, all bets are off. They have broken the ice and there is no going back. You just have to refer to the "male" sections of each example in the Appendix, to see what you will be stuck with. Just as when you buy a car, it always comes with wheels. You can't buy some used ones at a yard sale and show up at the car dealer saying, "Oh, don't charge me for the wheels, I brought my own." But, do not despair. Accepting that there are the "standard features" you will get no matter what, there are also some option packages. And, as with all packages, you might not like everything you get and there are always tradeoffs. But, you can make this work, if you manage your expectations properly and choose your package wisely.

Now I will talk about some of the Packages I am acquainted with and then I will detail some bonuses and red flags that can appear in any of the Packages, if not closely inspected prior to acquisition. Each Package has men of every ethnic background, race, religion and geographic location so, if that sort of thing is important to you, just use it as one of your "preliminary sorts". I do not claim this list of Packages to be exhaustive but more a reflection of those with which I am the most familiar. Hopefully it will give you a sense for how this works and you may uncover a Package that I had never even considered. I would be delighted to hear about it, if you were willing to share. Just make sure you don't mix up what is standard (you get it no matter what) and optional (you can find some models without).

The first Package we will look at is **The Intellect**. This guy can be very smart and well read. Often not as smart or well read as he believes himself to be but that is always relative to the audience. I mean every day we all run into people that are lots smarter than we, some of us recognize it and some of us don't. This guy is usually conversant on the Classics and Shakespeare, often speaks more than one language and can be found to know quite a bit about fine dining and rare wine. More often than not, **The Intellect** is well groomed and a sharp dresser, if you are fond of the *Brooks Brothers* and tasseled loafers look, and tends to enjoy the effect of pipe smoking. They can be somewhat fun-impaired, even a bit pedantic but, fun might not be important to you. Be careful if he slips his SAT scores or his college GPA into a conversation. This should not be important to an adult. It is usually a red flag that it is the last notable accomplishment he has had, at least by his personal measuring stick.

The Intellect is usually a name dropper but, often you have never heard of the people about whom he is bragging about being well acquainted with. Generally, there is an equal chance the person could be a current Nobel prize recipient or dead for two thousand years. If they have a single Greek or Roman name, the latter is more than likely the case. They tend to avoid anything more athletic than bird watching, firmly believing that "brains will always triumph over brawn". They talk about the "news readers" on the BBC as if they are personally acquainted and love to quote *The Economist*. This is the guy for you if you are fascinated with the orderly flow of world capital, the latest international coup or the current consensus of the implication of economic indicators.

Often they don't like to get dirty which is not necessarily a draw back, just something to keep in mind. My suspicion would be that they feel that sex can be learned from an instruction manual but, I have no first hand knowledge of this, it's only an impression I am left with each time I find myself talking to one of these guys for more than ten minutes. The fact that their hair is always perfect is, for me, a give away. How can you have really good sex with someone who is worried about their hair? That goes for both men and women.

These guys could be great if you were the type who always fell in love with your college professors or if you have always wished you had done some doctoral work but never had the time. They would be fun to travel with; you'd certainly never have to hire a guide. Planning is very important to the Intellect and they often lack spontaneity. However, I am well aware that many people do not enjoy doing things on the spur of the moment; in fact a well made plan makes many people quite comfortable. My only caution would be not to let him know you are as smart as he or, God forbid, smarter. That would be a deal killer.

The next Package is **The Workaholic**. If this guy isn't at work, he's talking about work and truly believes that the rest of the world is as fascinated with what he does as he is. He may or may not be clever, he may or may not make a lot of money but, boy oh boy, is it important to him to let everyone know, where ever he is, what he does and how good he is at it. This is the guy Palm Pilot must have had in mind when they came out with their prototype. He always has his cell phone with him and was brought to his knees with gratitude, when wireless e-mail was developed. They often begin conversation with, "Hey, I'm calling you on my cell phone. I don't have much time but. . ."

He has one excuse for not doing anything he doesn't want to do: "Sorry honey, I'd love to but, I've got to work." He feels he can be late for any event or pull a complete no show, without apology. He tends to be quite dismissive about anyone else's work, including yours (that is, if he even knows what it is you do), and has no idea what the expression, "get a life" means or how it could possibly apply to him. This is a guy who spends two thirds of the family vacation in the hotel room on the phone in conference calls that can not be interrupted, with his lap top on, speedily sending and receiving faxes. He generally arrives late and leaves early because, "he just can't be away". He has absolutely no idea what a stiff everyone, including his children, think he is. If he is aware of it, in some extremely perverse way, he considers it a compliment.

This is a great package if you don't really want to be married but need the income, if you really like to do things by yourself or, if you want complete control over the household and the children. This guy is way too busy to spend his time on fabric and wallpaper so, the house is all yours. He doesn't have time to make his own friends so, the social calendar is in your hands, unless he has a mandatory business event for you to attend. If that is the case, you must appear looking great and sounding intelligent. These events can actually be quite enjoyable; everyone in his office is very curious about "the wife", so you can really have some fun with that. Be creative.

He certainly doesn't have time to ride herd on your children so, you can usually decide how many you want to have and raise them anyway you want. You will decide what schools they attend, at least their lower schools, with only financial input and their cultural education will be in your hands as well. He usually presents quite well, at least on paper and the only time he will embarrass you is when he has bored all of your friends to death, talking about his job. That doesn't happen often because, he is usually at work.

All in, it's not a bad package, as long as you don't want any male companionship and can tune out someone who is boring you. Also, since this guy is usually too tired or busy to have sex, he'll never notice or probably even care with whom you are having it, allowing you a great deal of freedom.

Then, there is **The Artiste**. This guy is your sensitive, caring guy who is often extremely creative, loves poetry and is not ashamed to cry. This is a guy who will talk about his feelings to you and is eager to hear about yours. In fact, he will talk with you for hours about feelings, often crying. When you go to a restaurant he comments on the ambience of the room and appreciates the presentation of the food. Sharing a bottle of really good red wine with this guy becomes a cultural event. He is usually a fabulous cook and loves to entertain.

He will happily attend the theatre, opera or any museum opening, anywhere. When you go to a movie he never cares if there are subtitles, in fact, he prefers them. He will talk about the scenery, the costumes, the historical accuracy of the film and the cinematography. He is generally repulsed by violence.

When you pack a picnic to bring to an outdoor concert, he is delighted by your selection of cheeses and almost tearful over the foie gras. He can name most of the flowers in your garden and has good suggestions regarding the combination of colors.

He makes you cards and birthday gifts and loves to read out loud to you. He may even write his own poetry which he is happy to share. Their creativity usually rolls into the bedroom and they are great lovers. They consider it another art form, not a race to the finish.

This can be a really great guy if you don't mind a little whining. All men whine, these guys just do it a little more often. They tend to get a little PMSy.

This is a guy your grandmother loves and your brothers hate. He doesn't care though, because he thinks your brothers are philistines and is still getting over the fact your grandmother actually met Pavarotti.

These guys make A+ boyfriends however, a high percentage, but certainly not all, of these guys have trouble holding down a job, if they even have a paying job at all. I think the sensitivity and crying might have something to do with that. Be sure you check that out before you do anything permanent.

Another boyfriend, as long as you don't want to get too serious is, **The Life of the Party**. This guy is fairly self explanatory and everyone loves him. He is usually extremely witty and quick with the repartee and people are always recounting his antics. As long as you don't mind always being the designated driver, he can be fun.

This guy can be hilarious but beware, he doesn't like anyone else being the center of attention and will interrupt, or just talk right over, anyone who has the floor. This guy really needs a lot of attention and is easiest to take in a crowd. He has a built in switch and, when he is not the center of attention, he turns into a bear. He is definitely not husband material unless you are happy to follow him around and be his audience for the rest of your life. I would not recommend it.

Then there is **The Cowboy** (wonderful) – never to be confused with the counterfeit cowboy, **The Urban Cowboy** (horrible). We will cover both here but, you must be absolutely clear, there are in no way whatsoever, interchangeable.

Real Cowboys can be found anywhere, all over the globe.

However there are definite geographic concentrations, most notably in the U.S. in the South and Western part of the States. If you happen upon one in New York City, study him closely, he may be an **Urban Cowboy** – ICK.

You may be thinking, "Mimi, help me here. How will I know?" Well, what I am about to tell you may justify the price of this book all by itself because, I can not imagine anything in this entire world to be more disappointing than thinking you had yourself a real cowboy when what you had snagged was in truth, an **Urban Cowboy**. I could barely absorb a disappointment of that magnitude.

At first glance, for those of you who have had limited experience with cowboys, they make look very similar; each wearing hats, boots and, perhaps even a rodeo belt buckle. However, I assure you, they have no more in common than Neil Diamond and Neil Young.

First, look at the boots. A real cowboy is going to be wearing old, worn out dusty boots, which have never been polished. The heels will be worn down and, if you know what to look for, you will be able to find evidence that spurs have been worn with these boots. His levis will be worn smooth on the inside of his thighs and you will be able to tell by staring at his cute little behind that he has spent a fair amount of time in the saddle, with this particular pair of levis on.

Now, some of you out there, especially those from "The-Land-Of-It-Can-Be Bought", New York City, are thinking, "What the hell, anyone could buy those things. . ." I will tell you, these are just preliminary sorts. In other words, if you are looking for a genuine cowboy and you meet someone with shiny new boots and dry cleaned levis, just move along cause you ain't there yet. (I hope that I do not have to mention to you that, if he has on designer jeans, you best just bolt out the door. The same goes for a hair piece.)

A real cowboy never has his hair styled, always looks as if he is about 14 hours late for his next shave and his hands and fingers are really calloused. If he strokes your face with one of his fingers, he will apologize for how rough it is and will tell you how nice it feels against your very soft face. (At this point you are already gone, so you may as well enjoy the ride.) He would never ever have his nails manicured. In fact, he would prefer to have them pulled out, one by one, than subject himself to a manicure.

You may be thinking, I am still talking about cosmetic stuff. This can all be faked. Perhaps a beginner could be fooled by this sort of thing, although I doubt it. You see, there is something very different about someone who is very comfortable with what they have on as opposed to someone who is in a costume. It is an aura of sorts that just shines through. However, for those of you who still are doubters, there are a couple of things that can not be faked, not matter how clever the actor or how good the costume.

The first is the cowboy walk. This is a very fluid, partially bowed, but not anything you would ever call bowlegged, gait. (The only time I have ever seen anything, anywhere near like it, is watching a hockey player walk. I am not talking about when they have their equipment on, I am talking about after they have showered and changed. They have the slightly bowed look, along with the smooth gait. Don't be fooled. If you want to know if this guy is a hockey player, just ask him who was in the semi-finals of the Stanley Cup in 1973 – or any other year for that matter. If he looks at you and says, "Seventy-three? Oh yeah, that was the year that Montreal beat the Black Hawks in the finals. . . .we all watched that game at the Plow. What a series; Dryden won the Vezina trophy. . . .yup, that was 73 all right. So, that means that the Black Hawks beat the Rangers in the semis to advance to the finals. Why are you asking? Are you a hockey fan?" As he asks this question, he has tears in his eyes he is so overjoyed that he has found a woman who might consider an evening in an ice palace a legitimate date. This is not a cowboy, despite his slightly bow-legged gait, this is a hockey player. I am not saying this is necessarily a bad thing. It is just important to know what you've got yourself into.

Now that we are clear on that, let's get back to cowboys. You can not learn to walk as if you have spent your entire life on the back of a horse, when you are 35 years old and just hoping to get laid. It is utterly impossible and can not be faked. An Urban Cowboy will look like a full grown fool as he is attempting to saunter toward you and, unless you are really, really drunk, this will be very easy to spot. Maybe, if this guy went to acting school and studied under Clint Eastwood, he might be able to get the walk down. I seriously doubt he could fool me, but I have been loving cowboys my entire life. But, I will tell you something that can never be learned, faked or copied. Only a genuine cowboy can look at you with that crooked little half smile, tip his worn ole cowboy hat at you and say, "Yes Ma'am." Doesn't matter a damn bit what he is "Yes Ma'aming" you about girl, you are putty in his hands. (And that goes double for all of us Yankee girls – we can not possibly get enough of that

Ma'aming.) It's that crooked little smile that makes them look as innocent and in need of our help as any three year old child any of us have ever encountered. But, there is no way we have confused them with a child, being that they have on their dusty old boots, maybe a pair of spurs and their well worn levis, leaving us with nothing but pure lust in our hearts. It is absolutely overwhelming and we find ourselves reduced to barely being able to gasp "Where do I sign?" It is extremely fortunate that these men are not the least bit interested in any sort of material possessions. It was no mistake we all fell in love with the Marlboro Man.

If you are into fancy cars, forget this guy. He will be the proud owner of a pick-up truck. If you find yourself leaving with a man you believe to be a cowboy, and he heads toward a Lexus, run like hell. You have been fooled and are in need of some coffee and perhaps an eye examination. Just remember Joe Diffie singing his signature song, "Pickup Man". I always smile when I hear him singing,

> *"You can set my truck on fire, and roll it down a hill*
> *And, I still wouldn't trade it for a Coupe de Ville".*

Now that is a song written about a cowboy.

Cowboys love sex and seem to have boundless energy for any new event suggested; the more physical, the better. For the most part, they are very sweet and quite concerned about your enjoyment of each particular event. Although there are some who need to be reminded that sex is not just another rodeo event and that a fast finish does not give you a blue ribbon, from all I have heard, that sort of cowboy is in the minority. Most like a relaxing, slow time of things and, are in no particular rush to get anywhere. I guess I should mention here that they tend to be seasonally employed so, you may be finding his boots under your bed for awhile, especially if you are a good cook.

Cowboys also love to dance and will two-step you around the floor in a manner you have to experience to appreciate. Never expect him to do the twist or rock n' roll dancing for that matter but, once they hold you up against them and two-step you around the floor you won't care if you ever rock n' roll again.

They really appreciate a home cooked meal, especially if you have a griddle, and have no problems helping with the dishes. They can be pretty handy and will fix things such as a broken door or window. However, you can't be too fussy with how the finish product looks. These guys use rope, nails, duct tape and Bondo to fix any problem they encounter – and perhaps a little AR 200 after a trip to Mexico. They are not into esthetics. And don't forget, these are outdoor guys, so don't expect any help with your appliances.

Never start drinking shots with a cowboy unless you are serious, really serious about it. You will never win.

Unfortunately, I have no information about marrying a cowboy as neither I nor any of my friends have done so. There are many reasons for this, mostly we couldn't hold 'em down long enough, but if any of you are married to cowboys and would like to let us know what they are like as husbands, we would all be most appreciative. Is there any truth to that Willie Nelson song, "Mama Don't Let Your Babies Grow Up to Be Cowboys"?

We all have friends who have married **The Father Figure**. This guy is usually quite a bit older than you, but not necessarily. In either case, he will always act as if you are the child and he is the adult. He will take care of you for the rest of his life, giving you instructions on every aspect of your existence. Believe me, I have several friends who are very happy in this sort of a marriage. They love having a husband who will select their clothing, plan their vacations and manage their lives. They feel very good when they please him and they work very hard to do so. It gives them both great joy. These men are generally benevolent dictators, ruling their kingdom with love and generosity.

The thing that attracts you to this sort of a guy is how refined and genteel he is and unlike any other boyfriend you have had. He has had a lifetime filled with rich experiences and is eager to share what he knows with you. He may have a bit of Henry Higgins in him. Can you say, "The rain in Spain falls mainly on the plain?"

He holds the car door for you, helps you on and off with your coat and stands when you enter and leave the room. He reminds you of either your own father or of the one you wish you had.

Often it is not the first marriage for **The Father Figure** and he has very clear thoughts about what went wrong with his earlier attempt(s). In many instances he readily admits where he failed and can often be a very attentive, caring man. A lot of these guys take all of the complaints their first wives had and alter their behavior for the next wife. They are often nearing the end of their careers and have more time to travel and are much less enchanted with their professional success than they were in their earlier years. They are usually financially comfortable.

Generally **The Father Figure** does not want you to have a career. He may have been initially attracted to you because of your profession. You may have even met him through work but, once married he will want you to stay home. A board seat or two on the symphony or a local charity would be fine but, be prepared to leave your career. Not necessarily a bad thing, just make sure you clarify this up front. I must say that on many days, that sounds like a really good option to me.

Because most of them are "playing the back nine" (as my husband refers to being older than 50) they realize that life is fleeting and there is much to be experienced and enjoyed. They are open to learning new things and absolutely love seeing you naked.

Just remember, if he is 25 years older than you are, he may be taking care of you now but, you can bet the time will come fairly quickly when you will be taking care of him. Also, if you choose to have children, their father will always be an old man in their memory. Having said that, I must add that there are worse things than having a wealthy old guy for a father.

The next package I will discuss is the one with which I am the most familiar. It is called **The Boy-Boy** or **The Frozen Adolescent**. This is a guy that will join any competition, anytime, anywhere provided two things happen - uniforms are worn and score is kept. This is a guy who, at the age of 45, will proudly wear one of those t-shirts that says "My girlfriend or lacrosse?" on the front and "Where's the field?"

on the back. This can be a regional thing but, these guys always have a pair of skates in their trunk, along with a couple of bats, gloves, maybe a lacrosse stick or a tennis racquet, a pair of cleats and usually an extra pair of running shoes. In other words they are always ready to play. If they play hockey, they play in five leagues and think nothing of working all day and then driving two hours to a rink in some town you have never heard of. They actually believe that bringing you along and hitting a drive-thru Burger King counts as a date. This is the same guy that couldn't possibly drive a half hour to your nephew's first communion because it's just too far away. These guys can remember who scored a goal at a high school game thirty-two years ago at Lynn Arena but can not remember your birthday or the day you got married. Their idea of literature is *Sports Illustrated* and they have no compunction whatsoever about planning a weekend around the NFL draft. They talk about professional athletes as if they are personal friends or enemies and they scream helpful instructions to them as they watch them play on television.

Yes, the television is very important to these guys and they spend an inordinate amount of time watching it. All things being equal they would prefer to have at least one in each room of the house. It is the first thing they turn on each morning and the last thing they shut off. If you are smart you will not allow a television in your bedroom because a Boy-Boy believes he can do anything while watching a game. A Sunday in the fall revolves around the couch and football games – many, many football games. They can be professional games, college games, high school games - they would even watch neighborhood football if there were uniforms worn and score was kept. They refer to ESPN 2 as "the deuce" and would rather go without food than have their cable shut off.

These guys far prefer the company of other men to women. They are terrified of any sort of emotional commitment and have been known to stick their fingers in their ears and loudly repeat, "LALALALALALALALALALALALALA" when asked about their feelings. If they could, they would make their home in a locker room.

This is not a guy you bring to the opera, a poetry reading or any sort of cultural event where they may have to stretch. They tend to favor action movies and comedies, especially if the male characters have a lot of sex with gorgeous young women with unnaturally large breasts. Regardless of their age, they not only wear, but look good in, baseball hats.

What is the upside of this package? Well, they are usually very interested in sex, pretty experienced and actively participate with great enthusiasm. They seem to regard it as yet another competition and consider lacy underwear an appropriate uniform for your team. Because they flatly refuse to take anything seriously, they usually have a great sense of humor and are always ready for some fun. They love to show you how strong they are and are proud of the way they change a tire or put in your air conditioner. They get very excited if you make a big fuss about their muscles. If you enjoy cooking, these guys are your best audience. They could care less about cuisine — they like quantity. These are the guys who get really enthusiastic about meatloaf and become nearly orgasmic if you grill their hotdog rolls. They think spaghetti is perfectly acceptable to serve at a dinner party, as long as there is plenty of garlic bread. You don't have to worry about them becoming a vegetarian or being concerned about their cholesterol. Those are adult issues and will never be of any concern to these guys, no matter how old they are. They are big on desert and again it's quantity. Don't spend a lot of time making a chocolate soufflé; three dozen chocolate chip cookies would be much more appreciated.

If you like activity, these guys are great. Their idea of a vacation is one of constant activity during the day - tennis, hiking, skiing, kayaking, sailing, swimming, biking and lots of cocktails at night. If your idea of a vacation is reading on the beach, this is not the guy for you because they don't like to do anything alone. They insist on full participation in each event. These guys are great fathers as long as their children like sports but, they are not above cheating to win. I will never forget the Saturday afternoon our seven year old came into the house sobbing with frustration because my husband had "thrown out the invisible runner" because he (my husband) had been losing their game of invisible baseball.

They are the guys in the neighborhood who always are in the middle of a huge soccer, baseball or pond hockey game. They show your children how to hold a bat or swing a golf club, most of them have roller blades and love to play street hockey. Because they refuse to ever consider they might not still be 21 years old, they are always up for any type of activity or physical challenge and generally, are quite a bit fun to be around, as long as you don't mind being the only adult in the relationship.

A **Boy-Boy** is not threatened by your career. On the con-trary, he appreciates the fact that you have a job because it takes some pressure off of him and frees him up for more games. He is proud of your career and does not feel the least bit threatened about it because you don't wear a uniform and score is not kept, at least not in a way that he would recognize. And, finally, he truly believes, from the bottom of his heart that there is absolutely nothing in the entire world that can not be cured by a blow job, either given or received.

These are a few of the Packages that I know about. As I said, I would love to hear from you, if you can identify some that I have omitted. Remember that there are some things you can change and some that just come with the package. Look closely and determine exactly what you are getting.

Along with "the Packages" there are also some "Bonuses" and some "Red Flags" which can come with any Package but not necessarily. This may sound like common sense but, it is important to try to get as many "Bonuses" as possible and, when you spot a "Red Flag", just move on.

Because I am an inherent optimist, I will start with the "Bonuses". We usually associate this term with money received at work, at the end of the year. These are different and much more important to your personal well being. These are traits in your partner that don't disappear with time, like money or hair. In fact, most of them improve with time because, once the fabulous sex that brought you together loses a little bit of its luster, these traits move to the front row.

These, of course are listed in my personal order of importance. This is because I wrote the book and someone had to decide their order so, why not me? You will have to decide which of these is important to you and their order of importance.

1. A terrific father. You might say this is impossible to tell, before the man actually has children of his own. I would disagree. Just observe how he reacts to your friends' children and your nieces and nephews. Listen to how he describes his time spent with small children or how he reacts to the news that one of his good friends is about to become a dad. You will get a very clear picture of how he feels about small children. Some guys come around once they are actually part of the baby making process but, generally they revert to their old ways, once they realize that their talent is not unique.

2. Bright, good conversationalist, aware of what's going on in the world. My father once told me and, of course, I dismissed him entirely, that I should never marry a man who did not read *The New York Times* each day. He explained that, once all the "kissy stuff" wore off, there had to be something else there to keep me interested. I wish he had lived long enough for me to tell him how right he was.

3. Exuding great generosity and compassion. If I have to say more, we could never be friends and you would never understand anything I ever said to you or, the way I view the world. If you can, should still try to get your money back for this book.

4. Sexually adventurous with a desire for mutual pleasure. Make sure that he is completely aware that fore play is more than a concept that came out of the women's movement. If you work this right, it only gets better and better. You want

to find someone with an open mind and who is willing to try new things.

5. Sense of humor, ready to laugh at the world or himself. Never one to take himself too seriously – that could get so dull. They say that laughter makes you live longer. I have no idea if that is correct or not but, I could not imagine my life or my household without lots of it.

6. A good dancer. It doesn't matter if the technique is right, what matters is that they get out there and "dance like nobody's watching". Dancing can transport me into a good place no matter how blue I am feeling. I am fortunate to have a partner that is a pretty good dancer; in fact, on our very first date he announced to me that he was "the best dancer on the East coast." I recommend that you find one for yourself. It's something you can do together for as long as you live, where ever you are and, it doesn't cost a dime.

7. You can find a guy that's good looking, or, easy on the eyes, as they say down South but, that could be very fleeting. However it has been my observation that once a woman is crazy about someone, that person could turn into Jabba the Hut and they would still be looking pretty fine to their woman. We are so much more forgiving than men in this regard, I can't even begin to tell you.

I can't believe listening to some of the men I know, talking about women as if they (the men) are some sort of a beauty contest winners. I want to look at these guys and remind them that they are certainly not looking like any kind of an oil painting themselves, any more. And that is assuming that they were looking that good in the first place. Good Lord, don't these men have mirrors in their homes?

And now, we shall discuss the "Red Flags". Some of these are OK, something you could live with, to get other things you want or need. Some of these are signs that you need to pack your bags and run, baby, run. Those will be noted as such.

1. Cheap, or said in a nicer manner, slow to open his wallet. This only gets worse as time goes on but, if you don't mind, it is certainly something you could learn to live with. In fact, if you consider yourself to be thrifty, you don't want to hook up with a big spender. It would drive you crazy. Just remember, he will never be more generous than he is before you are married.

2. Bad Temper. Be real careful with this one. There isn't one of us that doesn't have some sort of a temper so, only you know if his is "bad" or not. It never, ever, ever gets better once you are married. If he ever hurts you, pack your bags and get out. It's just the beginning of much worse. There is absolutely no exception to this. Run while you are able to. There are people who will help you and places you can go. There is never any reason to stay in a place where you are fearful.

3. Bouts of unemployment. Depending on where you are geographically and how long they last, this could also be bad, unless you are content to be the sole support of your family. If this is the case, just work out his household responsibilities early on and make sure he is in agreement.

4. Never seen a woman he doesn't like. This only gets worse as he gets older. If you don't know all the reasons you should

leave this guy, there is nothing I can tell you.

5. & 6. These two go together because they are exact opposites. Too much of either can be a killer. A little of both is good.

Anal Retentive/Slob. An anal retentive or a real slob will drive you crazy unless you share those type A cleaning requirements or like to live in squalor. If either is the case for both of you, you will live together in harmony but drive all of your friends away.

No one likes to visit friends and be afraid to use the bathrooms or sit on any furniture for either reason; they are way too clean or way too dirty. If you can strike some sort of harmony on this, your life with be much more enjoyable. If you are at one extreme and he is at the other, best to shake hands and move on. With Oscar and Felix it was funny. If you had to live with that imbalance every day, regardless if you are the Oscar or the Felix of the group, you would lose your mind.

7. & 8. Like 5. & 6., these two are exact opposite and are best when you get a little of each. Either is a red flag is when one partner is one, and the other is the opposite.

No Friends/Never Met a Person That Wasn't a Great Friend. If he doesn't have any friends that is a bad sign for so many reasons it could be a book of its own but, for simplicity purposes, if he doesn't have any friends, he will want to spend all of his free time with you. (just think about what that means) There are reasons why he doesn't have any friends, be aware of what they are. Even the shyest guys in the world have a couple of friends.

Trust me, you don't want to be the woman who always has her man "just drop in" to Girls' Night Out. That is, if he even agrees that you should be going to Girls' Night Out. These guys always really frighten me. The whole control aspect is something I could never get with. At first it might be a little flattering that he doesn't want you out of his sight but, I would suggest to you that in most cases, it would become suffocating. Go really slowly with this; make sure you know what you're getting.

Then there is the guy with six million buddies that he can never disappoint when they call to ask him to him to go to an egg tossing contest or something equally weighty. All six million of these guys drink beer, lots and lots of beer and usually it is beer that you have bought, just to have on hand when someone drops by. They don't leave until it is all gone and, when your friends come by and you offer them a beer, there is never, ever even one left. If that's not enough to make you really dislike these guys, nothing will.

9. Avoid anyone who is a zealot, about anything. I don't care if it is the sport they play, or the church they attend. Unless you share this all consuming passion with them, you put yourself in danger of being consumed or left behind.

10. Be really careful of a guy who has a fascination with or has an unnatural attachment to weapons, other than those used in hunting. I recognize that this, to a degree, can be a regional thing but, there is no good reason for anyone to be mail ordering automatic weapons or rocket launchers. This is well in excess of what is covered by their "right to bear arms".

Something that you should think about, which is neither a bonus nor a red flag but something about which I am always surprised at how passionately women feel about is; their man's choice – boxers or briefs. What makes one man choose one over the other and why are women so passionate in their preference of one over the other? I have no idea but, I know women who don't care who the president is but have very passionate opinions on this subject. I have to say that I am strictly boxer shorts – preferably from Brooks Brothers. I couldn't exactly tell you why but, it would be definitely be a deal killer for me.

Decide if it is important or not to you and, if it is, use it as one of your preliminary sorts. I recommend you do this with some discreet questioning, well in advance of the actually seeing for yourself. This will prevent you from running out of his apartment screaming, in the middle of the night, trying to zip up your Levis.

Now the rest is up to you. I have given you the benefit of the collective wisdom, observations and experiences of all of my good friends and myself. There are people who spend thousands of dollars and years in therapy without ever receiving this high caliber of advice. This is a lot to think about I realize but, this is a very important decision, one that will truly impact the remainder of your life. Only you can decide when and who.

Just keep these two words in the forefront of your thinking:

• CHOOSE WISELY •

Combining Households

> "I'm not going to vacuum 'til
> Sears makes one you can ride on."
> -Roseanne Barr

As you approach the wedding you begin to look at the conditions in which your soon-to-be-husband lives and suddenly, you can't believe that you ever took a shower at his place or, God forbid, slept on those sheets. I believe it has something to do with the well documented scientific concept of "Love is Blind".

Whenever I hear someone suggest that, I have to smile as I recall Maisey telling me "Well, you know, love may be blind, but I can assure you Child, the neighbors aren't." I honestly believe this to be the sum total of my sex education.

When I met my husband, he had a great affinity for the color tan. It was all he owned. I never had any idea how many contrasting shades of tan existed, until I met him. He looked like a tree trunk – good thing he is so damn cute. Not only was every piece of clothing he owned tan but he actually owned, and I swear I am not kidding, tan sheets and tan plates. A former girlfriend had taken one of the tan sheets and made tan curtains. His apartment was a sight to behold. Fortunately, for him, it was very, very small. It looked like a little hobbit house.

The first Christmas we were dating, I bought him a really pretty blue cotton sweater. He has beautiful blue eyes and I knew it would look really good on him and, he could wear it with all of his tan trousers.

I was a little nervous on Christmas morning as he unwrapped this particular gift. He opened the box, looked up and said a bit tentatively, "Oh........it's blue." Fortunately his sisters were there and they immediately told him how nice it would look on him. He was not convinced and back it went, into the box and remained there for about a year. When he finally decided to wear it, lots of people complimented him, and each time he would nod his head, looking somewhat unsure and say, "Oh, yeah, thanks. It's blue." They would give me a rather peculiar look and I would just shrug my shoulders. What could I possibly add? It's refreshing to be dating a guy who knows his colors.

To say that he did not have a well outfitted home is an enormous understatement. After we had dated for a few weeks, we were sitting on his tan couch and deciding what to do for dinner. I suggested that, rather than get take out again, we could go out and buy some food and I would cook us dinner.

He wrinkled up his face and sucked in his breath, through his teeth and said, "Well. . . I don't know about that. . . "

I couldn't figure out what was up with that and, as I looked around his apartment (which took about two seconds) I asked, "What's wrong, doesn't your stove work?"

He glanced over to his tiny galley kitchen as if he was seeing it for the first time and said, "I'm not sure."

Understandable, after all, he had only lived there three years.

When it came time for us to combine our households, the contributions were a bit lop-sided. I owned a house. He had a hot air popcorn popper, a big ceramic bowl and a three-quarter quart Calphalon pan, to melt the butter for his popcorn, of course. I have no idea what happened to his tan plates.

This however, is a far superior situation than that of one of my friends who had to explain to her new husband that she did not consider painting on velvet to be art of any sort. I am not kidding. I have another friend who drew the line in the sand over having posters of the Boston Bruins in her living room. There is an advantage to marrying someone who lived as if he was homeless. Not only did he not bring along any preconceived decorating ideas, he was also extremely appreciative of having big fluffy towels to dry off after his shower.

There is a joke that a comedian tells, unfortunately I can't remember his name but he asks, "Did you never notice that single guys have the best parties? You know why that is? Because you can go over to their house, wreck everything they own, and they're only out $11." This could have been my husband, pre-marriage.

It's not easy to ask a guy like this to spend thousands and thousands of dollars on furniture, decorating, art and all the other things you must buy as you set up your home together. My advice? When he asks you how much anything cost, just look very vague and ask him what he would like for dinner. If that doesn't work, talk dirty to him.

It does seem that once you finally get things the way you want them in your house, it's time to start all over again. That is another really tough concept to sell to your husband, especially if he loves the chair with the holes in it.

Having a house is something that Americans strive for. It is part of the so called American Dream. Tax legislation has been crafted to help us accommodate this dream. But, what no one ever tells you is how difficult it is to keep this house clean or even picked up, once you actually get it. Paying the mortgage becomes the easy part, especially with all of the explosives we keep tossing in the air.

Sometime Things Fall Through the Cracks

I wrote earlier about the "Wonder Woman Complex", the belief that we could do it all. And we sure do try but, from time to time we are forced to face the fact that there are only 24 hours in each day and admit that some things just fall through the cracks. A physics professor would tell you with great certainty that a house is too big to fall through a crack, that is unless you live in California, but I assure you, it happens to my house on a regular basis. I can never understand how the work week can drag by so slowly yet, at home, the beds always need to be changed. This just isn't right. It's like living simultaneously in two different time zones, one where the time speeds by so fast you can see yourself age and another where everything takes places in slow motion.

And, I have another question – where does dust come from and how high would it pile if you never dusted? Is there a point where it solidifies and can be picked up and moved? I am actually conducting this experiment right now because I am certain that I am not the only person who has asked themselves these questions. If you were to drop into my house right now it would look as if no one had ever dusted any of the furniture, ever. Many of my friends are quick to point this out to me and, remain skeptical when I explain that it isn't a dusty house but rather a scientific experiment that I am conducting with the intent of selling my conclusions to *Good Housekeeping* for publication.

How about the women who keep their home so clean that people say, "You could eat off her floor." Well, if she is that tightly wrapped, she might actually want you to eat off the floor. How much fun could that be? Come to my house; it may not be sparkling clean but I will serve food to you on plates.

Have you ever noticed that with your first child, if anything ever comes close to the floor, it could never be returned to the child, without first being sterilized? By the third child, the twenty second rule is firmly in place. Maisey was certain that you had to "eat a peck of dirt" before it would kill you. I never asked exactly how much a peck is or whether it had to be eaten all at once to kill you or consumed over a life time of dirt eating. There are so many things I wish I had asked her.

Marian Heard, one of Boston's most respected and accomplished professional women is absolutely hilarious as she describes herself when, as a young bride, learning that her mother was on her way across town in a taxi, she flew into a frenzy, making the mad dash to clean her apartment before her mother arrived. She tells the story as one of the most formidable fund raisers in the city, in her role as CEO of the United Way. She is such a together woman, the epitome of confidence and cool, she has her audience howling with laughter and disbelief, just trying to imagine her not completely in control of her entire universe. Women like Marian are very generous to share stories such as those with us, helps us to set our expectations.

It's amazing how we can take comfort in this sort of story. My friend Bonnie's mother is a woman for whom I have enormous respect. She is truly one of the most refined, lovely women I have ever known and I consider her to be a wonderful role model. She is always impeccable, as is her home. She remembers everyone's birthday and always takes the time to send a card, with a really nice note. She is one of the most gracious hostesses I have ever known and she has a lovely sense of humor. She has a garden that could be featured in *Town and Country*. Each time I would visit her home, I would feel totally intimidated, feeling that this was a level I could never even aspire to.

Then one day we were talking and Bonnie was describing one evening when she was in high school and was taking a bath, her brother, whom I also know, rolled in a cherry bomb that exploded, while she was in the tub. When I asked her mother about this, expecting her to deny it or say that it must have happened when she wasn't there, her mother just smiled and shook her head as she recalled the event. Oddly, I took a perverse comfort in that story knowing that, if this sort of thing could happen in her mother's home, my household wasn't as out of control as I sometimes feared. Or, maybe it is, but I am not alone.

Light bulbs, toilet paper and toothpaste are the glue that holds a household together. I would submit that the person who buys them is the one who is in charge because without these items, the household falls apart. If you don't believe me, just rid your home of this stuff and see how long it takes for chaos to set in.

When we were first married my husband told me one of the things he liked best about me (he is a real romantic guy) is the fact that there were always spare lights bulbs in the closet, when one blew out. I asked him what the big deal about light bulbs is and he told me that they might have been the second greatest source of the battles between his siblings and him, after who got into the bathroom. When I expressed my disbelief, he explained that when he was growing up, if a light bulb blew out, he would just go into one of his sisters' rooms and take one of theirs, not the least bit concerned if it would leave them in total darkness. It's a miracle they still like him.

Energy and Force Fields

I do believe there is a certain energy or force that runs through your home, causing things to happen over which you have no control. In the Introduction I talked about *The Dryer Effect*. Where do all of those socks go? Why do people just blindly accept the fact that over their lifetime two-thirds of their socks will never make it out of the dryer? Don't you think it odd that we can send people to space, have them orbit the earth a few times, take a few pictures and bring them home safely yet, no one has even attempted to find those socks? I think someone knows where they are and it is closely tied to our national defense. Otherwise, why wouldn't they just tell us?

Another baffling force I have observed is the one that determines that once, one of your major appliances dies, the rest follow, one by one, in a very short time span. And why am I usually out of town on business? I can't tell you how disconcerting it is to be in a huge client presentation and get called out to receive a phone call from one of your children saying, "I think the refrigerator is broken. All of the ice cream has melted and is oozing out the door." Like Clark Kent, you have to mentally jump out of your business suit, into your Wonder Women outfit; remember the name and telephone number of the appliance repair person, call him and beg his mother (who manages his appointments) to please send him to your home immediately because you are in Chicago and there is ice cream squirting out of the freezer; jump back into your business suit, return to the meeting with a big smile and try to regain your thought process, all the while thinking about melted ice cream being tracked throughout your entire house.

Am I the only one who wonders exactly how does your dyer find out that your dishwasher just died? They aren't even in the same part of the house. It's uncanny and there is absolutely no relationship between the day they were purchased and the day they died. The only relationship to the purchase date is that they always survive three days longer than their warrantee, regardless of how long it has been extended. It is a force that takes over your home and one by one, they all just crap out on you, often right before or directly after the holidays. Just try telling little kids that this year the family Christmas gift is going to be a washing machine. Good luck with that.

And then there is *The Hamper Effect* which is the phenomena where you spend all of Saturday emptying all the hampers in your home, doing countless loads of laundry, running up and down the stairs so many times you feel like a fitness instructor and then, when you go into everyone's bedroom to put the clothes away, the hampers are again overflowing with dirty clothes, some of which you have never even seen.

This is a force or effect that I am particularly interested in understanding because, if I could harness this force and redirect it to my checking account, it would be great. Can you imagine, spending all day Saturday emptying your checking account and, at the moment your money is all gone, it fills up again? Who cares if the money needs to be washed? Hell, I would wash and iron it if necessary. I am working on this and, once I have it figured out, I will write another book and let you all know. Until then, I will be spending my Saturdays running up and down the stairs, doing laundry.

Have you ever wondered how you can spend hours carefully studying those little tiny strips of paper with paint colors on them, select a very soft, almost white, shade of pink and then, when it is applied to your walls it looks as if there was an explosion of Pepto-Bismol in the room? I refer to this as the "exponential acceleration of color" and it's just one more of those mysteries that everyone calmly accepts. I believe there is a close connection between this phenomena and the Union of Interior Decorators but I haven't been able to uncover any evidence of illegal activity yet.

First You Take Out Your Glue Gun

When you are trying to manage your family, home and career, it is easy to become intimidated by those women who seem to be able to do everything perfectly. We all know at least a few of these women and they intimidate (actually, they scare the shit out of) all of us, men and women alike. We all suspect that we could probably arrive at their home, unexpectedly, at 3 AM and they would greet us at their door, with their hair and make-up perfectly in place, and dressed for entertaining. I don't need to tell you, if you have read this far, should you ever arrive at my house at 3 AM, you will be most welcome but not only will I not be looking too good, more than likely, I will have really bad breath. If you expect anything other than being directed to an empty bed, you will be sorely disappointed. If you are really fortunate, the sheets will be clean.

Even though I accept that I am not one of those women that can make a fabulous Christmas gift from a toilet paper tube, I am always open to learning something. One of my much younger buddies, Lisa, (actually she is the daughter that I never had), asked me to go to one of those house tours with her; where, if you pay a little bit more, you attend a little lecture where they guarantee that you will be able to make all of the decorations that you have seen throughout this designer house. I have to admit up front, we were skeptical.

After we enjoyed the wonderful house tour, we sat down in a lovely room and listened to two, very energetic sisters, describe to us how they easily made all of the decorations we admired as we toured this house, practically in their sleep. Lisa and I got really excited because they were using words like "quick" and "simple". All of a sudden, this sort of thing appeared to be within our reach. We were practically high- fiving each other as these sisters told us how easy all of this is to do in your own home. Then, faster than we had gained our confidence and before we could even feel smug, it was snatched from us as she looked us in the eye and said "The first thing you have to do here is to take out your glue gun...." Lisa and I looked at each other and wondered if we could get our twenty dollars back, both realizing that if the first assumption is that we owned a glue gun, we had no chance whatsoever to proceed to the second step. Give me a break, I have never met anyone who owns a glue gun unless they are a teacher at an elementary school.

Our fears about step two were confirmed when the other sister said, "And then grab the box that is filled with all those ribbon scraps you have saved all year." Lisa and I looked at each other and started laughing. Could it be possible that we were the only people in the room without our own glue gun and box of ribbon? We realized that we had to get out of the room before we were discovered to be imposters. We were afraid they may string us up with their ribbon or shoot us with their glue guns.

I have to confess that it took me a long time to not feel totally inadequate whenever I would receive an incredibly creative, artistic homemade gift. It is so far beyond anything I could ever do, it just boggles my mind. What kind of person goes into the woods and finds perfectly symmetrical pine cones or sucks out the insides of an egg through a pin hole? Isn't there anything else they would rather be doing?

I understand that Martha Stewart is a working woman and I believe she was even a single mom but still, you have got to be kidding me. She is probably a lovely woman but I suspect it would be really tough for me to warm up to anyone who knows how to apply gold foil. There is just something unnatural about it. I should come clean right here and tell you that I am not exactly sure what gold foil is and for what purpose it would be used but I heard her talking about it on her show once when I accidentally turned the television to that station. It is still unclear to me what purpose it serves. I have determined that it is not a fancy alternative to aluminum foil but I haven't progressed beyond that in my research.

Have you ever looked at her magazine? I'll bet she owns about ten glue guns, especially if they come in more than one color. I know, you think that I am just jealous, knowing that she is one of the wealthiest women in America but, that's not the case. Sure, I would like to be one of the wealthiest women in America but I would draw the line at sucking out the insides of an egg through a pin hole.

As much as we all would like to be able to do everything perfectly, at all times, there are choices we must make. And, it is very important for us to not only be realistic in our expectations but also to know our personal limitations. Do not consider it a failure on those times when you have to say, "Sorry, I just can't do it."

Having a house or any dwelling for that matter is an experience that is always expanding, no matter how large or small your house is. Everything I know about electricity or plumbing is due to the fact that whenever even the smallest thing goes wrong, we have had to pay someone to come in to diagnosis and repair the problem. Some women are very handy; some have husbands who are very handy. My good buddy, Arden, and I have Al. I have to be honest and tell you that Arden discovered Al and, being the good buddy that she is, she shared him with me.

To call Al a miracle worker could offend some people and believe me, that it not my intention but, to me, that's what he is. I recall the time I ordered a desk from a catalogue, for one of my children. The description in the catalogue did say "limited assembly required" however, it would seem that I took the word "limited" too literally. When the truck pulled into my driveway and these two muscular guys jumped out, I thought, "Great, here comes the desk." When they each grabbed a very long, but extremely thin cardboard box, I marched right out the door to tell them they were mistaken. I had ordered a desk, not some flat thing. They very politely put down the thin boxes and referred to their clip board. It seemed I was the one who was mistaken; these two narrow boxes, with approximately 1,956 screws, washers and other assorted hardware I had never even heard of, contained the makings of a desk. Once I got over my shock, I called Al. Two days later we had the fanciest desk you have ever seen. If we ever move, I am going to try to sell it with the house because we could never get this thing down our narrow staircase.

Al is a guy you can call with any sort of a household problem, describe it to the best of your abilities and tell him the door will be open. You can then go to work or, if it's the weekend, do your 2,483 "weekend errands" and when you come home, Al has fixed the problem(s). Al really likes Arden and me and he can not fathom how it could have possibly happened that we are both married to men who play golf, rather than fix the screens on the porch, replace the garage windows the kids have shot out with hockey pucks or stop the kitchen faucet from having water shooting out of each side. He has, on occasion, spoken of each of them in a very derisive manner. He has even suggested that Arden and I could have done much better with our spousal selection.

Dick, who owns the hardware store downtown, tends to agree with Al on this subject but, Dick really has to be pressed to give his opinion on someone's husband. In fact, it would not be an exaggeration to refer to Dick as reticent in this regard. Arden and I have tried to interest him in teaching a class called something along the lines of "Household Management 101 for Husbands Who Never Took Shop". He merely laughs and refuses, shaking his head and suggesting we contact his wife with regard to his qualifications. However, Arden and I are pretty sure that, despite anything his wife could possibly say to us, our husbands could really learn a lot in this course. What Dick fails to realize is, he is the glue that holds many marriages in my town together, with his consistent, calm advice and problem solving skills.

Although Al regularly tells me what a schmuck he thinks my husband is, Dick really never said anything to me until I came in and bought the chain saw. I think that frightened him, even though it was the smallest chain saw he had for sale. He asked me who was going to be operating this chainsaw and, when I told him that it would be me (I am not a large woman), he just shook his head with an uncomprehending look on his face.

I started laughing and said, "Don't worry Dick, it will be fine. I lift weights. Besides, my husband is out playing golf and someone has to clear out the back yard." He didn't say much but, what he was thinking was written clearly on his face. Dick and Al are in agreement, Arden and I could have done much better.

But, we forgive them because, Al and Dick don't play golf and, with all due respect to these fine men, they could never understand *The Golf Effect*, which actually gets its own chapter, coming up next.

The Golf Effect

"Give me a man with big hands, big feet and no brains and I
will make a golfer out of him."
-Walter Hagen

Things can be really moving along nicely, your job is going great, you and your partner are just clicking, really enjoying one another's company, looking forward to the time you can spend together. And then, something always comes along and mucks things up.

One of my theories of why a relationship is so difficult can be viewed as sort of an economic concept or analysis. That is, in most relationships there are two limited or, in a pure economic sense, scare resources, time and money. There is often such a struggle trying to reach agreement on how each of these scare resources will be utilized or, in more practical terms, spent; that much of your free time together is spent arguing about these issues. This is not a good thing. This does seem to be a nearly universal phenomena, by that I mean that most of my friends have also experienced it.

Each winter, a sort of harmony sets into my household because, the free time that we can spend together, although limited, is pretty easy to agree on. As a family we really like to ski. We enjoy dining out or having friends in for dinner. In New England, things slow down in the winter; you can actually find yourself snowed into your home without power for a day or two. Providing that you have ample candles and flashlights, this is not always a bad thing. A certain sense of adventure takes hold and, at least for a day or two, we all recapture some aspect of our pioneer spirit. Snowmen are built, complete with the carrot nose and the red plaid scarf. There is sledding and skating and everyone feels invigorated and quite healthy. It's almost like a vitamin ad.

Then the warm weather that we have been waiting for for the past six months arrives and everything goes awry for those of us who have husbands who play golf every waking hour, returning home only to be fed and get clean clothes. It defies any rational explanation. There have been times, in the middle of a particularly grueling tournament, that my husband did not appear one hundred percent certain which children were ours and which were guests, as he rushed in for a dry change of clothes. Sometimes I feel like one of those guys in the racing pits that has to change the tires really quickly on those racing cars, so the driver barely misses a minute of the race.

Meanwhile, as our men are single-handedly keeping golf the most popular sport in America, we run the household, which includes everything from grocery shopping, cooking, cleaning, changing beds, transporting children, decorating, entertaining, ...well, you get the idea. We are not stupid women so, you find yourself asking, "How can this be?" There is a very rational explanation. It is *The Golf Effect*, which was briefly discussed in the Introduction to this book. If necessary, go back and review it now so you won't be totally confused.

It is because of this very force of nature that otherwise competent women, accept without question, the fact that their husbands feel perfectly justified, spending every daylight hour of the weekend on the golf course, not to mention the money spent, but it would be crass to bring that up. They generally arrive home after several beers, famished, and announce they are far too tired to go to the auction you have been working on for the past six months or any such social event that doesn't revolve around the men he just spent the past twelve hours with. Also, although they have absented themselves from the home since first light, the moment they arrive home, they insist that you are there, with a full course gourmet meal prepared. They don't care what you were doing or with whom you were doing it while they were gone but, once the king returns to the castle, the queen must be there, looking quite spiffy, to pay proper homage and provide sustenance.

There is a joke going around on the internet about golf and every woman I have told it to, thinks it is a riot so, I am going to share it with you.

As is his habit each Saturday and Sunday, a man goes out to play golf, really early in the morning, despite the fact that the weather is just atrocious. It is raining, sleeting, and even hailing. As he makes the turn, it is so cold he can't even feel his hands so, he reluctantly heads home. He gets to his house, makes himself some coffee and turns on the weather channel, only to find out that, as the day goes on, the weather is just going to get worse. Being a prudent man, he decides to make the best of a bad situation and very quietly goes up stairs to his bedroom, where his wife is still asleep. He takes off his clothes, slips into bed and, as he nuzzles up to her he says, "Can you believe that it is raining and sleeting out there? There is even some hail."

She smiles sleepily and relies, "Can you believe my husband is playing golf?"

For some reason unknown to me, none of the men I tell this joke to think that it is even the least bit funny.

It is also *The Golf Effect* that causes them to believe that, when we ask how they played, just to be polite, that we are interested in hearing about the game, not just hole by hole but rather, club by club. An example: "Well, I got to seven, you know it's the dog- leg." He says this knowing full well that I have never been on the golf course, (actually I was on the golf course once but, it was at night and I had had an industrial quantity of wine, so it really doesn't count) "And I took out my five wood but, then I remembered that six weeks ago, Billy drove the green with his seven." This is a man who can not remember to stop and get milk on the way home but he can remember the club, used by one of his friends, in a golf game six weeks previous. "So, I took out my seven, looked at it, but put it back in favor of the five." Please note, he has not yet hit the ball, even once. Believe me when I tell you, it takes less time to play a round of golf than to hear one played. The only answer I was looking for was either "great" or "crummy".

Actually, I don't even have to ask how his game was. It is written all over his face and he comes up the walk. If he has on his "dink-face", we all run for cover, not wanting to hear, for the 620th time, how he is quitting the game and taking up gardening. If he is smirking, in a manner that has been much maligned in our new President, GWB, we know we are in for a long and boring retelling. And, if he virtually skips up the walk, we know that we are going to be hearing all about his new golf swing and how this will be the year that he wins the club championship. I'm not sure which one is worse.

Whenever I remind him that H.J. Whigham advised us in *The Common Sense of Golf*, written in 1910 that, "The most important thing for golfers of all ages and handicaps is not that they should play golf well, but that they should play it cheerfully," he looks at me as if nothing would give him greater pleasure than to kill me with his bare hands. At that moment I am aware that the only thing that saves me is his fear of being confined in a small space. Perhaps the conclusion we should draw from this is that common sense and golf are, indeed, oxymoronic.

The Golf Effect caused one of my friend's husbands to think she wouldn't mind that he planned a trip to Scotland, with a bunch of the guys, five days after she gave birth to their third child. He was incredulous that she objected to being left alone with a new born and two small children and he couldn't understand how his passport could have just disappeared. The men were unanimous in their diagnosis. . .must be some post partum hormonal imbalance. He went to Scotland and she didn't kill him when he came home. Only a force of nature could account for such events which would otherwise defy any rational explanation.

On this same golf trip to Scotland, obviously under "the effect", one of the players thought his wife wouldn't mind if he charged a $2,000 kilt to her American Express. I should probably mention, this particular husband was not employed at the time, with no funds of his own. Thus proving, *The Golf Effect* is an international force.

My own husband, standing right in our kitchen, undoubtedly suffering from "the effect", thought that he could convince me that he CERTAINLY HAD told me (with the emphasis on certainly) he would be going to Hilton Head for a week with eleven other guys. They were leaving the next day. You can believe me when I tell you that would not be something I would forget.

Sometimes you have to fight fire with fire. The next day, I went in to work and asked my secretary for some help which, once I explained the situation, she was only too happy to provide. I asked her to find me a place where I could take the children that would be warm and preferably, not too expensive. Oh yes, and we would be leaving the day before he returned. I left a nice note in the kitchen. . . ."As I told you, we have headed down to Aruba for a week. See you when we get back", signed with a little smiley face. I seemed to have made my point. I now receive ample notice prior to all golfing boondoggles.

Another thing I noticed is that "The Golf Effect" can cause one to loose perspective. One of the coldest Januarys on record up here in the Northeast, my husband and his friends took their "January Golf Trip" to Palm Beach. I think they figure if they call it that, all of their wives will think that they have to go, it being January and all. Anyway, while they were gone we had the coldest ten days, of the coldest month on record. As if that wasn't bad enough, my youngest child got the chicken pox and then, our pipes froze and we had ice dams everywhere. I had water squirting out of the most unlikely places, all over the house. It was below zero, I had a sick child and no heat in the house. At seven o'clock in the morning, the plumber and the oil service man were both standing in my kitchen, trying to avoid getting drenched by the water pouring out from everywhere. The fact they were there at such an early hour was a direct result of the hysterical message I had left each of them at 4 AM, when I first heard water pouring into my downstairs. The telephone rang and, the husband whom I had not heard from in four days was on the other end of the line. As I began to recount to him all that had transpired in his absence, bordering on hysteria, he thought that it might be all right to say, "You think its cold up there, well, it's cold down here too and my putting is in the hopper."

Even his golfing friends thought that he was a little bit over the top with that one. There can be no other plausible explanation - another clear example of *The Golf Effect*. The plumber and oil service man, who are not golfers and therefore not aware of "The Effect", were suddenly quite alarmed and were afraid they were going to have to call someone with a straight jacket to contain me. All of a sudden, my broken pipes seemed to take a backseat to the hysteria that appeared to be setting in as I broke the receiver of the phone, smashing it down. But, to fully understand how completely irrational *The Golf Effect* can leave people, you must hear the end of the story.

Two days later, which may not seem like a long time to you as you are reading this but let me tell you, it was like two days of dental work, my husband called again. To see how his son was? No. To see if the pipes had been repaired and his family had heat? No. He was calling to see if I would pick him and some of his golfing buddies up at the airport. You are wondering if I did it, aren't you? I'm going to let you wonder about that.

The Golf Effect has been documented to have affected the judgment of at least one of the presidents of the United States. William Howard Taft is acknowledged to be the first U.S. president who was a golf enthusiast – his predecessor, Teddy Roosevelt, "The Rough Rider" felt golf to be a sissy sport.

Taft is quoted as saying, "The beauty of golf is that you can not play it if you permit yourself to think of anything else." You've got to wonder where his spin doctors were when he was shooting his mouth off about not thinking about anything other than golf. It is claimed that he even snubbed a foreign head of state saying, "I'll be damned if I give up my golf game to see this fellow." to the White House messenger who came to tell him that he had company. I guess the guy should have phoned ahead. We can only hope that he played golf as well, so he would not feel slighted.

When Dwight D. Eisenhower was president he was so wild about golf that he had a putting green put in at the White House. Stephen Ambrose tells us that one of Ike's greatest sources of frustration was the squirrels who would steal his golf balls and hide them. He had his secret service guys catch them in have-a-heart traps and release them at Camp David. Yet another example of your tax dollars hard at work. Good thing for Ike that Ralph Nadar wasn't around then.

It is agreed that John F. Kennedy was the most skilled golfer to serve as president of the United States and Gerald Ford most likely the worst. Ford was quoted as saying, "I know I'm getting better at golf because I am hitting fewer spectators." There spoke a man with his expectations in line.

Richard Nixon, who had never seemed like a real fun guy to me, had the putting green removed. But do not despair, it was restored under the presidency of our most fun-loving president to date, Bill Clinton. Robert Trent Jones, Jr., a leading golf architect, told then-President Clinton that, "building a putting green at the White House should actually be considered a restoration." Is he kidding? This is exactly what I am talking about when I refer to *The Golf Effect*; it causes otherwise normal people to say and do the most peculiar things.

I should mention that the restoration of the White House putting green did not cost the taxpayers a cent. All machinery, materials and manpower were donated. To be the best of my knowledge, no one involved received any sort of a presidential pardon so, it was all for the love of golf, and the idea that a golfing president is a happy president, once again illustrating the universal nature of "The Effect".

As you can imagine, I have talked to many women about *The Golf Effect* and I have to tell you, they are so grateful for finally having an explanation for that which defies any other explanation, they fall over themselves, thanking me and then begin to share their own stories. It boggles the mind.

One of the nannies whom our family employed over the years had a boyfriend who went on an overnight golf trip with his buddies. This boy was remarkable only for how stupid he was so, the upshot of his golf trip did not entirely surprise me. He ended up with a broken leg and poison ivy, from head to toe, on every imaginable place on his body. When I asked her how this possibly could have happened, she explained, if such things can indeed be explained, that one night after, one can only imagine how much alcohol was consumed, they decided it would be a good idea to drive around in some golf carts, naked. Well, this genius managed to drive his golf cart down a hill, breaking his leg in the process and landing in a field of poison ivy. When his friends informed him that he was submerged in poison ivy, his response was to begin pulling out bunches of it, throwing it in the air and yelling, "Poison ivy? Exceeeellllllleeeennnnt!!". (This took place shortly after the release of his favorite movie, *Wayne's World*.)

I mention this incident not because I think *The Golf Effect* played any role in it whatsoever. I am not even sure golf was played. Where "The Effect" enters into this story is, after I repeated the story to my husband, waiting for him to be as shocked and appalled as I with regard to these events, he calmly turned to me and said, "Well, yeah, I could see that happening. Poor bastard." You can be sure, I did not inquire further.

In my efforts to provide a complete picture to you, I did some international research of my own on the topic. You just can't trust the stuff the government has done because, from what I can see, almost everyone in Washington is a man who plays golf; not exactly what I would call a group of impartial observers.

What better place to conduct this sort of research than the golfing capital of the world, Ireland? According to The Irish Times, in the year 2000, 235,000 traveled to Ireland to play golf, of which only 19% were Americans. Given this fact, I believed that this would be a great place to expand my nascent research project, on *The Golf Effect* and draw my final conclusion with regard to it's international reach.

So over I went and, when there, I met a lovely couple from Dublin. Before long we were talking about golf, not as a game but as something that impacts a relationship. Sally, the wife, was relating to me that her husband would soon be going to Spain, with ten other men, to play golf. I asked her if she would be going along and she looked positively shocked by the suggestion and replied quite emphatically, "I should say not. I know these men and, I suppose, each of them by themselves can be quite nice but, in a group, with golf in mind, they become something entirely unattractive. And, they suffer under the great misperception that, just because they also play also bridge, they are civilized."

As she was telling me this, it was clear to me that, in her mind, this defied any sort of logic or rational explanation. That settled it for me; *The Golf Effect* is without geographic borders. The inclusion of bridge on a road trip is definitely regional.

As I was explaining my hypothesis to them; John, the husband, was looking at me as if I were just another weird American, but Sally was nodding in complete understanding and feeling appreciative that she no longer had to be concerned about the dramatic changes she witnessed in John's personality whenever golf was involved. She obviously took more than a small measure of comfort with this explanation and I felt happy, knowing I had done a good thing. Sally has promised to expand our grass roots movement and spread the word to women throughout Europe.

People are often amazed that, given the amount of time that my husband spends playing golf, I have no interest in taking up the game. When I watch the range of emotions that he goes through, doing something he supposedly loves, it is not the least bit mysterious to me. I would have to be absolutely out of my mind to do so. This is not something new. Even William Shakespeare understood the mercurial emotions brought forth by this game. In *Richard III* he writes, "Cursed be the hand that made these holes."

Although my husband claims that he loves the game and, indeed, he certainly does take every waking opportunity to play it, golf is the single greatest, consistent source of frustration in his life. Even more so than that posed by either the children or me (pay attention to the word consistent here).

I recall talking with him when he was on one of his January trips and when I asked politely, "How is the golf going?" he reported that the new, extremely expensive driver he had received for Christmas had suddenly, for no apparent reason, broken. I was not pleased in the least hearing that I had purchased a defective club. I assured him that I would call the golf shop where I had purchased it and get him a replacement. There was a pause and it was only then that he mentioned that he had "just tapped it against a tree".

"Tapped?" I asked incredulously, "Why would you ever tap one of your golf clubs against a tree?" He did not have a reasonable explanation. I suppose I should find some measure of joy in the fact that he didn't claim to have been trying to "tap" a little bit of dirt off the club head.

Fortunately I decided to wait until he got home before I assaulted the golf shop and, this was the correct decision. Unfortunately for him, his brother was also on the trip and when I asked him for his interpretation of events, after he stopped laughing, he managed to say, "Tapped it? That's what he said? It was more like Babe Ruth winding up at bat."

I wish I could report to you that this was the last of the broken clubs. One of the positive outcomes of doing the research for this book was that it has been affirmed to me that my husband and late father are not the only people to take leave of their senses while engaging in, what I have come to call, "the act of golf." There are thousands, if not millions of examples of this and narrowing down the field of those to share with you was not easy.

However, when I came across the "Temporary Rules of the Richmond Golf Club," written in 1940, I decided that they so clearly illustrated how *The Golf Effect* causes otherwise rational, intelligent individuals to think in a way that defies any sort of explanation, I had to include it. Can you imagine being at the table when this rule was written? I can not begin to visualize the conversation of which this was the outcome. I am guessing that large quantities of alcohol were involved. There is no other plausible explanation for this temporary rule, even recognizing it was written in 1940.

"In competition, during gunfire or while bombs are falling, players may take cover without penalty for ceasing play. The positions of known delayed-action bombs are marked by red flags at a reasonably, but not guaranteed, safe distance there from. A ball moved by enemy action may be replaced, or if lost or "destroyed" a ball may be dropped not nearer the hole without penalty. A player whose stroke is affected by the simultaneous explosion of a bomb may play another ball from the same place. Penalty, one stroke."

I rest my case.

In fairness to my husband, I have to say that I did not have a particularly pleasant introduction to the game of golf. My father was in almost every instance, a gracious, compassionate, generous, mild mannered man, with two exceptions: in a sailboat race and on the golf course. In each instance he turned into someone barely recognizable and not particularly likeable. This was more than likely my first introduction to *The Golf Effect*, I just was not aware of it at the time.

Although he believed in his heart of hearts, that women should not be allowed on the golf course, he accepted, somewhat reluctantly, that this was a situation beyond his control. With this in mind, he felt it was his duty to teach me how to play golf because he believed that he owed this to my yet undesignated husband. It was not a pleasant experience of either of us.

My birthday is in July and he thought it would be grand if, for my 16th birthday, he made it a total golf birthday. To this day, I can not conceive how he possibly thought this would be a good idea. Not only did he buy me new clubs and shoes, he went over to Mark, Fore & Strike and bought me a hideous green skirt with a frog on it and matching peds, with lime green balls on the back of them. I nearly threw up. Then, as if this wasn't enough, he decided the two of us would play golf together. It may have been the worst idea he ever had.

When I say things were going from bad to worse I am not exaggerating in the least. He turned in some sort of a golfing Ahab, shouting orders and instructions, as if our national security was at risk. He was really wearing me down and, let's not forget, it was my 16th birthday. Why didn't he just take me out and shoot me?

As with all terrible situations, there is a final scene. My ball was in the woods again, no surprise there to Ahab, and about 20 feet away from one of those gigantic old trees that long ago split in half and had grown into a giant V. If I were to hit my ball straight, it would have sailed directly through the center of the V however, Ahab ordered me to aim at the left trunk. I suggested to him that, due to the fact that it was a straight shot to hit it though the middle, aiming at the left trunk was a questionable plan. He then exploded and announced, "You couldn't hit the side of a barn if your ball was directly in front of it. Aim left, you have been hitting right all day long."

I thought to myself, "All day long........it's only been a day?" It seemed to me that at least a week had passed. I glared at him and said, "FINE." as I walked up to the ball and whacked it as hard as I could, aiming at the left side of the tree

Sure enough, didn't my ball hit the left side of the tree with the force of a nuclear blast and, much to the horror of both of us, ricocheted off and came screaming back, directly at my father. I should mention that my father was nearly six feet, four inches tall and weighted about 230 pounds; in other words, he was not a small man and made quite frightening picture as he dove to the ground, all the while yelling it was entirely my fault.

I probably don't have to tell you that after this, all hell broke loose. Although I would have not thought it possible, he became even more irrational and accused me of actually trying to hit him. When I explained to him that it was he who had devised the strategy of me aiming for the left side of the tree trunk, he actually had the unmitigated gall to suggest that if I had indeed aimed at the left side of the tree as instructed, I would have missed it. Things were really heating up and, I may have even accused him of being the worse father in the entire world, suggesting that I would have quite a good case for Protective Services. His answer for a very high percentage of my complaints was, "NONSENSE!!!" and this was what he shouted in response.

Well, it was my birthday and I had had enough. I marched up to the green and took my brand new golf bag, filled with my brand new golf clubs and made my best attempt to scatter them as far as I could. I then took off my brand new golf shoes and threw them at my father proclaiming, "I hate this stupid game. It is for idiotic old people and I will NEVER play it again."

Although I think he was secretly relieved I did not also take off that horrid green skirt with the frog on it, he gave no indication of any sort of good feeling and, as I was marching off and he was demanding, in his most authoritative bark, "Come back here right now. You MAY NOT walk off of this golf course. . . come back here, right now. . . RIGHT NOW. . . ."

I marched back to the club house with tears streaming down my face. This was beyond anything I could have ever imagined and, at the time, something from which I was certain I could never recover. The one thing that I may not have made clear is, I adored this man and the fact that this entire debacle had occurred my "Sweet Sixteen Birthday", made it all the worse. I had spent a great deal of my life, up until that point, just trying to please him. Obviously I was missing the mark and given the way I was feeling, I was certain it would have been preferable if he had just shot me. But, of course, this is the thinking of a hormonal sixteen year old.

Our club had a small back balcony and, on sitting on it having a martini was my Uncle Jack, my godfather, who also happened to be my father's brother. He saw me coming down the hill barefoot and sobbing and called to me, "Bad round, Princess? He has always been an asshole to play any game with. Let's really piss him off. Come on up here and I'll buy you a beer, it is your birthday, isn't it?"

I'll bet every single one of you reading this, wishes you had an Uncle Jack. I can tell you, all of my friends wished for the same. He was a treasure and I still miss him.

Any one who knows this story never asks me why I don't play golf.

It's a Good Thing They Are Born So Cute

"Why am I so soft in the middle
when the rest of my life is so hard?"
-Paul Simon

Now you're married, sharing living space and both of you are working away at your careers. You have each staked out your side of the bed and there are no longer any bad feelings about who got the red toothbrush. If you want to have pancakes for dinner or, no dinner at all, that's up to you. You have night after night of uninterrupted sleep and if you want to get away for the weekend without any advance planning, your only obstacle is reservations. You can walk around naked and have sex in any room of the house, any time you find yourselves there together. Yup, life is good.

Then, one day, for no apparent reason, you decide to throw a wrench into this idyllic scene and add a new family member. A baby no less; someone who doesn't even have a job and who not only won't be contributing to the household financially but, will turn into the greatest financial drain you have experienced to date.

As I have previously stated, there is not a universally right time to make this move and you can always find a million reasons not to. In fact, in the face of this multitude of negatives, it is nothing short of a miracle that the population continues to grow.

But, there are plenty of reasons why we have our first child. Babies are popular. Your parents really want you to have them so you can find out firsthand how awful it is to raise rotten unappreciative kids. They also want to have an ally or two when they feel like ganging up on you and an eager audience when they recount all of the transgressions you committed while growing up. The federal government is in favor of babies, they even give you a tax deduction when you have one. And, with this financial windfall you could take your newly expanded family to Burger King. The National Organization of Babysitters wants you to have babies. If you don't, their members will no longer be employed, causing great a disruption in the cosmetics industry. And finally, your friends and relatives that have babies want you to have them so you can all be poor and sleep deprived together. They are always saying things like, "What's the matter, is he shooting blanks?" making you eager to prove them wrong. You don't realize, until you have children of your own and you find yourself asking your childless friends the same question, that it is all part of a plot, perpetrated by the powerful lobbying group, the UBW, which is of course, the United Babies of the World.

You never make the decision to have your first child with any sort of realistic expectations. No matter how ready you think you are, how long and to what degree of detail you have planned for the event, you will still be blindsided. In fact, the more organized, structured and in control that you are, the less likely it is you that you have anticipated, even remotely, what it is you have undertaken.

Please don't misunderstand me here. I absolutely love being a mother and my children mean everything to me. I could not envision my life without them. However, I was totally unprepared for how changed – albeit, for the better – my life would be. I was accustomed to being in charge; a decisive decision maker; the person who made the plan. All that flew out the window once my first child was born. All of a sudden my entire life was subordinated to someone else's needs. This was something that took some getting used to. It was well worth it though. I can't imagine undertaking anything else so difficult, yet so rewarding.

You do have to wonder, shouldn't there be some sort of a test you have to pass before you can have a child? Until I became a mother, I had to score really high on one or more really big tests, some of which took all day, and then compete like hell against a pool of other interested parties any time I wanted anything. But not with babies. You show up at the hospital in the middle of the night and they just hand you a baby and wish you well.

I recall after my first child was born wanting to ask someone, "Are you telling me that you are just going to give me this little baby? He can't even walk or feed himself. Does he come with a change of clothes? What's he going to do all day when I'm at work? By the way, what's his name?" It was more than a bit overwhelming when I realized the nursing staff would not be coming home with me. I am surprised that the Democrats haven't found a way to regulate this.

One thing that works in your favor is that their memory doesn't kick in until they are three or four so you can screw up lots of times and they don't remember. Even if they have some vague, memory of being dropped or slipping under water in the tub, you can always say dismissively, "Don't be ridiculous, you were only one when you claim this happened. You couldn't possibly remember back that far." When you are stating this, I would recommend sounding very sure of yourself. They are experts at spotting weakness.

Of course this will only work for your first child. Once you have more than one, the older ones become the permanent recorders of their parents' gaffs, often blowing the stories way out of proportion. When that happens, it becomes your word against theirs and, we all know how people love to believe the worst about anyone, but especially about their parents.

One of my very good friends is an extremely organized, very successful professional woman. She is in charge of a very large corporate division, with many employees and a great deal of responsibility. She is accustomed to being the boss.

Before her first child was born, she and her husband had thought of everything, even names. They had hired a nanny from Ireland to care for the baby when they were working. The nursery was beautiful – decorated for a princess. They had bottles and diapers and miniature furniture of every sort you could imagine and could have opened a store with all of the toys and beautiful little outfits they had. There was nothing that they did not consider and plan for. I was really impressed because, by contrast, I always felt as if I was flying by the seat of my pants and, quite honestly, compared to them, that is always the case.

They had a beautiful baby girl. I remember seeing her, shortly after the birth and will never forget her saying to me, with great enthusiasm, "I love it. It's just great. The best thing is, nothing has changed. We bring her everywhere. And, I already have her on a schedule."

As I stared at this adorable baby girl, sleeping peacefully in her $400 wicker carrying basket, lined with Pierre Deux fabric, I found myself wondering how could this very bright, well educated, sophisticate be so deluded? Of course, I realized that it would only be a matter of time before she was disabused of this foolish notion and realized that no one ever wants to sit next to your baby in an expensive restaurant, even if you bought her dress in Paris, and the only people who will be on a schedule will be the parents and the nanny. But for the time being, I let her believe this. And why not? After all, she is a good friend and, what can be gained by spreading bad news?

One thing I have noticed about the young women I know who are now having babies is, they read lots and lots of books. I think this is great, after all, information is power. They know what to expect each day of their pregnancy and are alert to any exception. When I was pregnant with my first child, the only baby books, in addition to Dr. Spock and Dr. T. Berry Brazelton, were those which gave you guidelines on "Non-sexist Childrearing". Don't laugh, for those of us who came of age in the 60's, this was critical.

There are times though when I wonder if all of these books might provide a false sense of security to the reader; a sense that they have been briefed on any eventuality that might occur once they have a child. I can assure you, there are not enough books in the world because the one consistency with children is, they will always surprise you.

There are also events or situations that, even if you were to read about them, you would not be prepared to experience. One example of this is the total lack of privacy you have, once you have a child. At my house, any time I enter the bathroom, for any reason, everyone in my family lines up outside the door to ask me urgent questions such as, "Where are my running shoes?" "Did you get my skates sharpened?" "Do you think we will get much snow next winter?"

I refuse to answer any of their questions or engage in

conversation with them, the only result being for them to repeat their questions louder and with a greater sense of urgency. And people ask me why I work.

I remember slipping into the bathroom one evening, hoping for five minutes alone to paint my toenails. What was I thinking? I was not in there 20 seconds when one of my children materialized outside the door, demanding to be let in. When I refused, he started slamming himself against the door and wailing, "Let ME in RIGHT NOW." I spent a week with four toenails, on one foot, painted.

This is the same child who, from the time he was two until he was four, no matter where he was in the house or what he was doing, if he heard me drawing bathwater, he would take off at a full tilt boogie, stripping off his clothes while at a full run; something I hadn't seen done since Winter Weekend at Dartmouth, many years earlier. There was absolutely no chance of talking him out of joining me, regardless of what I promised him. I challenge you to show me a book that tells you how to shave your legs with a three year old sitting in your lap, insisting on washing your hair.

It is amazing how quickly they figure out all the things that make you feel guilty and utilize them with abandon, to make you feel worthless. When I returned to work and, as a result had to stop breastfeeding, my new baby just stopped eating. He would fast until I got home from work. As you might imagine, the poor thing was absolutely famished each night by the time I got home. There were nights I could hear him screaming when I drove into the driveway. I was growing more frantic by the day, ready to just give up and quit my job. Had there not been a seriously negative financial implication with that solution, I suspect that's what I would have done.

Our pediatrician suggested that I go into work later in the morning, allowing me to spend some extra time with him and to feed him his breakfast. I would get ready for work, then put him into his highchair and try to feed him his breakfast. This is one of those situations that sounds much more simple than is actually the case.

He was a very determined child and insisted upon feeding himself and also insisted I remain there for the duration of the meal. His method of feeding himself consisted of picking up one Cheerio at a time, staring me directly in the eye, placing it on his tongue and waiting until it dissolved. Do you have any idea how long it takes to eat even ten Cheerios in this manner? Try it sometime. This was absolute torture, sitting there, trying to look cheerful and supportive of his eating.

My extensive research has uncovered the fact that food is first definitive weapon your children learn to launch at you. I am ashamed to admit to you how clever I thought I was with my first child, who would cheerfully eat anything offered to him. I had the mistaken idea that it had something to do with my great maternal skill and found myself feeling quite superior to my friends who had to bribe or cajole their children to eat. I think I may have even said something insufferable such as, "Well, if they are hungry enough, they'll eat it." Hopefully I didn't compound it by adding something ridiculous such as, "Who is the adult and who is the child?"

The gods do have a way of leveling the playing field and my

next child fasted. He also went an entire year where he ate only grilled cheese sandwiches – breakfast, lunch and dinner. You can't even imagine how ridiculous you feel in a restaurant asking the wait staff if the chef could possibly be persuaded to make a grilled cheese sandwich for your three year old child's breakfast. First they look at this little blond boy who sweetly, but unapologetically, smiles at them and then they look at you as if you are the most pathetic excuse for a parent they have ever seen. I don't care how smart you are, how much money you make or what a big deal you are; your children will make you humble.

While we are on the subject of small children, I would like to ask the crowd, who the hell came up with the term, "the terrible twos"? I would venture it was either someone who was not a parent or who had completely lost their mind by the time their children had become teenagers.

After all, with a two year old, as challenging as they can be, you have ultimate control. But that I mean, when nothing else is working; when they refuse to respond to all of your best efforts, some no doubt gleaned from the myriad of books you have read; you can always pick them up and physically move them; albeit at times amid some vigorous kicking and screaming. I am not claiming that it won't be embarrassing but, you are ultimately in control when you can move them from one place to another. Not only that, a two year old can not drive and, in spite of all of my vigorous international research, I have not been able to uncover a single documented case of two year old pouring tap water into a bottle of Grey Goose vodka or using their parents' credit card to fly themselves and some friends across the country to see a PHISH concert. Now we are talking terrible.

We like to think of each of our children as uniquely talented and gifted with skills far superior to those of their peers. Although each of our children does indeed have many endearing traits that are unique to them, their also share many similarities. It is the similarities that tend to frighten those parents who are honest enough to acknowledge they exist.

The same child who will selflessly volunteer to feed the homeless, night after night at the local shelter, will still leave their soaking wet towels on the bathroom floor and the sink filled with their dirty dishes. They think nothing of taking the last dollar out of your wallet or drinking every single drop of the Johnny Walker Blue their father received as a 50th birthday gift. After all, someone drank all the beer. Can you guess who that was?

Let me also caution you, their hearing is selectively bionic. They often don't hear things that you say to them when you are standing six inches in front of their face, such as, "Will you please pick up the wet towels you left on the bath room floor?" but, when you and your husband are behind closed doors whispering, they hear every word and repeat it back to you at the worst possible time. The same is true for their memories. They can not remember to put the trash barrels in after school, even though this has been their responsibility for the previous six years, each Monday afternoon but, just say something, anything about your mother-in-law and they remember it forever, reminding you from time to time that they have not forgotten and are just waiting for the right time to spill the beans.

SOMETIMES, THE TRUTH HURTS

Don't waste your time worrying about them embarrassing you with things that aren't true, regardless of their age, they use the truth like a saber. One of my friends nearly died when she was at her mother-in-law's home and her three year old daughter looked up from her Barbie dolls and said, "Mom, Grandma's not an asshole." My friend, being a very quick thinker, decided to pretend she had not heard her daughter and hope that her three year old attention span would kick in and she would be on to the next topic. No such luck. Not only did her daughter repeat her observation much louder this time, my friend claims that she had never heard her annunciate so clearly.

This is another one of those situations where there is absolutely nothing you can do or say and precisely what my friend, Sally, has in mind when she reminds me, "You know Meemz, there is a very good reason why some animals eat their young."

I respond by telling her that the legal consequences for eating them are too great to make it attractive. (I don't even bother to get in to what it would do to our social standing in the community.) Rather, what we have to do is to merely write these events down to insure that we will remember them and, at a much later date, take the opportunity to embarrass them to the same degree. I assure you, just as I assure Sally, they will present ample opportunity to do so.

I grew up in a rather formal household and many of my friends have heard me say that the only body parts that were identified or talked about were those you could see when you had on a snowsuit, to include a hat and mittens. Like many of my friends, we vowed that we would have a much more open, relaxed atmosphere, where anything could be discussed without embarrassment. There was also a great deal of discussion on the terms that would be used to identify our private parts. There was a shared feeling of contempt for the practice of using anything other than the biologically correct terms. Then we had children and reality set in.

One of my friends was in Bloomingdales shopping with her daughter who was about three or four years old at the time. As my friend was shopping, her daughter was engaging a rather natty looking gentleman in conversation. He appeared to be in his late 60's or early 70's, and was sitting there, waiting for his wife to make her selections. My friend was watching her daughter carefully and could clearly hear their conversation. It was all the usual sort of things that you would expect: her name, how old she was, if she went to school, etc. Then there was a lull in the conversation and, much to my friend's horror, she heard her daughter state quite clearly, "My mommy has hairs on her pachina."

My friend was absolutely horrified and wanted to climb into the rack of dresses and just hide there. The poor man was stunned and unable to respond. He eventually just got out of the chair and staggered away. We can only guess what he suspected must go on in my friend's home. This caused all of us to rethink our position on the naming of anatomical parts, a decision that was affirmed for me when my three year old asked our 72 year old neighbor if she had a "hoo-hoo". With a perfectly straight face, I told her a "hoo-hoo" was new kind of ice cream pop. I do hope she never asked for them at the grocery store.

It's a Good Thing They Are Born So Cute

We all have mortifying stories of the conversations our children had with strangers, in our presence. I recall bringing one of my children into the bank one afternoon when I had too much banking to do at the ATM. He was about three years old at the time so, I sat him up on the counter while I was filling out my paperwork. When he was very small, he found that if he said to someone, "I like your hair." or "I like your blouse." he received a wonderful response. The recipient was both surprised, as well as absolutely delighted, that this sweet, tiny child had paid them such a nice compliment.

As I was filling out my papers I was not surprised to hear him chatting away with the teller, a lovely woman, I would have guessed to have been in her late 50's. What I was not prepared for was when he looked directly at her and said, "I like your bosoms." I nearly died. I did not acknowledge what he had said, I just grabbed him off the counter and stood him next to me. The poor woman was so flabbergast, she could barely complete my transactions. There was, of course, absolutely nothing I could have said.

That evening I realized what at least half the problem was. As I was recounting my embarrassment to my husband, his response was, "Well? Was he right? Did she have nice tits?" Sometimes I feel as if I am swimming against the tide. . .

Having children is an adventure for which you can never prepare. Having children and working full time can test the limits of your sanity. When my first child was a baby, I had to take a business trip out of town. I got a ride to the airport from a friend of mine and she came in with me to wait for the plane to take off. Because she was taking care of my son, he was with us as well. We were sitting there chatting, and I noticed a little girl who would walk a few steps toward me and then go back to her mother. Her mother would urge again toward me.

After I watched this happen a couple of times, I caught her eye and said, "Honey, do you want to see the baby?" turning him around in her direction.

She recoiled from him somewhat, shook her head and said to me in a really little voice, "My mother said to tell you that the baby threw up all over your back."

Sure enough, it wasn't merely down my back and all over the suit I had to wear to my meeting but it was also in my hair. It is amazing to me that you can become so accustomed to an odor that unique, it doesn't jump right out at you, especially as it is spewed down your back. I think it was my perfume for about ten years.

One of the many things that continues to amaze me about babies is, how their output can be so proportional greater than their intake. By my calculation, for every four ounces they take in, they expel about two pounds. It makes the concept of adult diapers truly frightening.

SOMETIMES YOU JUST MISS

My family and I have always lived in a small suburban town where the majority of the mothers, at least those with young children, "were stay-at-home moms." Because I have always worked, I often felt like some sort of a freak and it was reinforced by the town, the mothers, the schools, the media and even my own children.

One morning as I was racing out of the pre-school one of the mothers stopped me and said in a rather accusatory tone, "I don't know you." I just looked at her, said nothing and continued to run down the stairs toward my car. She demonstrated her sharp powers of deduction as she looked at me and said quite contemptuously, "Oh, you are the one that works."

I slowed down enough to say, "who works. . . . I am the one *who* works, not *that* works." I am sure reinforcing every rotten thing she had already decided about me.

You never want your children to feel disadvantaged so, if you are ever doing anything different, you worry about the effect on them. I felt awful when picking my son up at daycare one day, he asked me why I was the only mother who didn't wear fun clothes. I told him it was because I worked and they played tennis but clearly, it would have been his preference to have had me showing up in work-out gear. I can't describe how defeating that feels. You find yourself questioning everything you are doing and how it relates to your priorities. Believe me when I tell you that the lines are far from clear and that they vary from day to day. Here we have yet another thing they neglect to cover in business school.

And why, oh why, is every school play held at 11 AM, making it impossible to go into work, if you have any sort of a commute at all and, really shooting the shit out of your afternoon? This is all to see your child dressed as a carrot, with two speaking lines. I can't tell you how many times my carrots, I mean my children, announced that they were the only child there without a parent in the audience, completely forgetting all of the times both parents were there, wildly applauding and encouraging the parent audience to do a "body wave". And, shall we talk about trying to make the carrot costume? I don't know why it is just assumed that I would have an orange body suit or anything suitable for the green stuff on top. Add to this, my kids only tell me they need a costume at eleven o'clock the night before they need it.

My friend, Candy, will laugh for the rest of her life, each time she thinks of my youngest son in one of the school plays in his costume. People like Candy are not only extremely organized but also, extremely creative. This could never happen to her.

As we are going out the door to school my son announces, "Oh Mum, I need a white sheet for the play we are doing today, in school meeting."

That's just great. He's in a play that, once again, I know nothing about and therefore, won't be in attendance. Also, I don't have any white sheets, none. So, son-of-working-mother will arrive without his costume. It's only 7 AM and my head is already pounding.

Then I remembered that my older son came home from prep school with a white sheet, still in the plastic wrapping, that his roommate's mother had bought for his roommate. How my son arrived home with it was never explained to me. But, I was grateful as I raced up stairs, dug through the linen closet where I thought that I had stuck the sheet and was ecstatic when I found it.

There were two things that I did not realize. The first was that he would be wearing this across his forehead like some sort of sheik and secondly, it was a fitted sheet. Candy absolutely dissolves into hysterics describing my son, with a fitted sheet attached to his head, with all the other second graders with long flowing robes. I know this is the stuff my kids will talk about when they are in analysis.

Because things like this happen, when we do know about something, there is the tendency among working mothers to over compensate. When one of my children was in pre-school, once a month you had to provide the snack for the class. As I rushed in one morning with the fruit and cheese tray that I had put together about midnight of the previous evening, the teacher said to me, "Oh, that's a thing of beauty. I just love it when the working mothers have to bring the snack. They always go overboard." I thought about her comment the entire way to work, trying to decide if I was pleased or pissed off. I could never decide.

I was having lunch with one of my clients who is a trial attorney and we were discussing this very thing. She had me howling as she was describing the afternoon she took off to help make scenery for one of her children's school holiday plays. She confessed to me that she realized that it was probably a good thing that she worked because she almost came to blows with another mother over the all important topic of how many cotton balls should be glued onto the cardboard snowman to make him look authentic.

And what about Halloween costumes? This is something that you have to witness before you are ready to believe it. The entire holiday (or, is it just an event?), turns into a cut throat competition among the suburban housewives. I have often wondered: is Halloween actually a holiday? I'm not sure.

Although I know Hallmark would say yes and I remember that it was the Feast of All Souls and a Holy Day of Obligation, making attendance at Mass mandatory, I am not sure about official holiday status. My determination of a holiday is merely this: do I have to go to work or not? And, unless Halloween is on a weekend, the answer is yes, I do have to go into work, disqualifying it as a holiday and making it all the more difficult to pull off. Do you realize that there are suburban towns where you can not buy those giant bags of candy after five PM, a fact which has caused me to be frantically driving around to adjacent towns, desperately trying to find an open store, with candy that meets the approval of my family. One of my friends, when faced with the same situation, decided she would just give out dollar bills. That was until she realized the same kids kept coming back. She then just shut off her lights and hoped they would think that she wasn't home.

Because of this competition and my frantic obsession that my children not be any different, despite the fact that I work, I could have never allowed them to wear store bought costumes. That is until the year one of my sons insisted on being Mr. T, from *The A Team*. After trying every possible combination of things I could think of, I finally admitted defeat and brought him to the store where, amid the cheap and garish polyester and plastic, we miraculously found the actual Mr. T. costume. He was delighted and I was enormously relieved but completely unprepared for his assessment when, as we were driving home he announced, "Finally, a real costume." I about drove off the road.

PURPLE HAZE IS IN MY BRAIN

Sometimes you suffer under an illusion that you are in control but generally you know that each day, someone or something is being neglected. I refer to it as the "Who-Gets-Screwed-Today?" conundrum. (I actually thought about using that as a name for this book but I was afraid it would scare off a few buyers, perhaps thinking it was some sort of business porn manual.) You can't focus on it though or you would cripple yourself completely so, if you don't opt for pharmaceutical relief, you often operate in a type of self-delusional haze. The haze is only temporary because there is always some event that forces you back to reality.

You know you are in trouble when, as you are frantically racing through the grocery store, throwing things into your basket with the hope of having some approximation of a healthy family dinner that evening and you see someone from your child's school who, when spotting you, bursts out laughing. This happened to me when my oldest son was in the first grade and I saw a friend of mine who also happened to be the school system's psychiatrist. You can probably appreciate why the school physiatrist may quite possibly be the last person you want to be telling what they believe to be a funny story about one of your children.

My efforts to hide in the bread display were not successful and she walked up to me, still laughing and saying, "I have to tell you what happened today. . . ."

I shamelessly tried to say I was in too much of a hurry to talk to her but, she was insistent, clearly feeling this was too good not to share. This occurred back in 1986 when the schools were trying very hard to create awareness in the young children with regard to AIDS, drug and alcohol use and inappropriate sexual activity. They were launching some pilot programs and my friend, Carol, was there in her capacity as a psychiatrist, attempting to gauge the appropriate level of information to provide to the lower school students.

It seemed that the message given to this age group was "choice", an offshoot no doubt of Nancy Regan's "Just Say No" campaign. The school nurse, the principal, a doctor and a police officer each talked about the choice the children had in a situation where they were offered alcohol or drugs or if someone was touching them in a way that made them uncomfortable.

The police officer was wrapping up and he closed by saying, "Just remember kids, you always have a choice. You can always say no." Then he asked if they had any questions.

Carol was sitting in the back of the room and she saw my son's hand shoot up. The officer called on him and was shocked as my son announced, "No sir, I don't have a choice."

Carol said the police officer was a bit shaken, clearly suspecting that in their first presentation they had uncovered a child who was being abused but he kindly said, "Yes son, you always have a choice."

My son politely, but very matter-of-factly stated, "No, no I don't have a choice. My mom told me that if I ever took drugs she would kick my ass all over town."

Carol said that a much relieved police officer, trying very hard not to laugh, replied, "Sounds like you've got a pretty good mom."

You must be careful what you say to them because, despite your best intentions, there is always the possibility that it will come back to bite you. Not unlike the situation a very good friend of mine found herself in several years ago. She was living in a very posh suburban town and claimed to be the only single mother who lived there. I would use her name but she would kill me because she is all married up again and pretending to one and all that she has never been divorced. Her secret is safe with me.

It was the holiday season and her young son was going to spend Christmas with his father. Because he still believed in Santa Claus, they celebrated an early Christmas together the previous evening, with her telling him that Santa would come to both houses. With that in mind they set out a snack for Santa however, it was not the traditional snack. She explained to her son that Santa probably got sick of all the milk that people left for him and, given how cold it was outside, wouldn't it be a much better idea to leave him a glass of scotch? He agreed and so, they set out a nice glass of single malt and off he went to bed.

That should have been the end of the story but no such luck for her. The next evening, as she was racing through the grocery store with him (perhaps we should just stay out of grocery stores) her son spotted a Santa Claus, half way across the store. Now remember, Christmas was still several days away so, when her son yelled across the store, "Hey Santa, how did you like that scotch my mom and I left out for you last night?", she was certain that every woman in the store glared at her as if she was the biggest tramp they had ever seen. Right when she was thinking that she could not possibly be more embarrassed, Santa yelled back, "It was great, tell her I'll be by again tonight." It's no wonder she got married again.

After a while, you get skilled at weighing the possible consequences of them repeating anything you have said, and pretty much stop talking in their presence. But after awhile you develop a false sense of security and let your guard down. This is the only excuse I can give you for the following story.

When my youngest child was in preschool we were going through the interviewing process for the next school he would attend. My husband and I had already decided that he would go to the same school his brother was attending, as we were very pleased with the school. However, my sister-in-law suggested that we also have him apply to another local school because, for the $40 application fee, they did a pretty comprehensive neuro-maturational evaluation of your child.

I had taken the morning off from work to bring him to his interview and was sitting in the living room reading the newspaper when my older son came downstairs. He asked me why I was still home and I told him about the interview. He very indignantly said, "He's not going to *that* school, he is going to *my* school." I assured him that would be the case I just wanted him to go through this evaluation. I had no idea bionic man was listening to this conversation.

We were at the school, sitting in their living room and the Director of Admissions came in and introduced herself. She then asked my son if he would like to go down the hall with her to play with some of the things at the school. He very politely replied, "No thank you."

She looked at me, a bit surprised, but remained calm. I spoke to him for a minute or two and persuaded him that he should go with her, assuring him that I would be here waiting for him. He agreed that he would do so and I thought that I was firmly in control of the situation until, as he was walking away with her I heard him say, "There is something you should know. I am not going to this school, I am going to my brother's school. I am just here because my mother wants me to take your test." I have no idea if she looked back in my direction or not because I frantically opened my newspaper and held it up, in front of my face, the moment I heard him say, "There is something you should know." I was stunned when he was accepted to their school.

Although I would never suggest that either my children or yours have ever made themselves sick on purpose, I do have to wonder why it is that on the night before the most important client meeting you have ever had, one that is pivotal to your career; one of your children will get sick and you will spend the entire night ferrying between your child's bedroom, the bathroom and the laundry room. As you dress to go to work, only because you absolutely have to attend this meeting, your child looks at you bravely through their glassy eyes and says in their little two inch voice, "It's ok Mum, I know how important your job is." Right, why don't you just run a stake through my heart?

You try to explain to them that you wouldn't be going if you weren't absolutely certain they will be fine after they have a chance to sleep (there's that word again) and if the meeting wasn't extremely important. You say this with a confidence that you don't feel and burst into tears as soon as you get into your car to race to the airport. Of course you are running dangerously close to missing your flight because your overwhelming sense of guilt caused you to leave your house much later than prudent.

You make your best effort to wipe the smeared mascara off of your face and try to catch a little bit of sleep on the plane. This is rather difficult because all you can think about is the sick child you have left at home.

You arrive at your meeting, a boardroom filled with men, each of whom have had a full, restful night of, yes, sleep and think to yourself, "Am I completely off my rocker?" This, of course, being strictly a rhetorical question, you are not required to answer it.

The entire time you are making your presentation, analyzing the volatility of the capital markets and fielding your clients' questions, you are asking yourself what kind of mother would leave a sick child at home and fly to New York? You find yourself speculating on the degree of psychological damage you have inflicted and you conclude he may not even want you at his wedding.

The presentation is finally over and you are ready to pack up and race home. Suddenly, out of absolutely no where, your client stuns you by announcing, "We would love to have you join us for lunch."

You can not believe what you are hearing. You have worked with these particular clients for six years and they have never even wanted to have a bagel with you. You are incredulous; the only time you absolutely have to catch the next possible shuttle, they want to eat. How can this be? God must be a man.

What do you do? You go to lunch of course, all the while having a vision of the department of social services driving away with your sick, sobbing child; as you try to force down a chicken Caesar salad and make small talk.

As you make your way to the airport, four hours later than you had planned, you find yourself feeling once again, that you have let down everyone in your life. You close your eyes, your head is pounding but, you are far too exhausted to cry.

You've Come A Long Way Baby, Maybe

"If you can't be a good example,
then you'll just have to be a horrible warning."
-Catherine Aird

I am certain that you have realized, as most of us have, that things are seldom what they are cracked up to be. One instance where this is painfully true is traveling for work. It is not glamorous, even if you are one of those *Sports Illustrated* models in Bali, working on the famous swimsuit issue. (OK, OK, I am just guessing here.) Work is work and you are always tired at the end of the day. You don't go to the museums or fancy restaurants, unless you are with a client and you never get to "see the sights". You don't want to and, even if you did, there is never enough time. You get there, do your work and leave as quickly as you can. This is not a vacation, it's a job. Lurking in the back of your mind there always is the fact that your family is home, needing you to be there.

Unless you own your own company or work for someone like Goldman Sachs, you don't get to stay in fancy hotels so, the beds are never comfortable, the pillows are always like rocks and the people in the room above you sound as if they are break dancing all night long. If you are lucky, you won't be able to smell the previous occupant's after shave lotion. I was in a hotel room once and the guy who stayed there before me must have taken a bath in Brut. I hadn't smelled that since high school but, it is a unique and unforgettable fragrance. All night long I kept thinking I was at the drive-in.

It's bad enough traveling for work when you are single. You ramp it up fifty fold once you get married and have a family. Regardless of how far we believe we have come, there are still clients who say things like, "You must make a whole pile of money. I would NEVER let my wife go to Texas without me. I suppose he doesn't know you are having dinner with ME?" And then he leers at you.

It's enough to make you lose your lunch on the guy, right there, as you realize that he still considers himself to be an object of desire or, maybe he thinks that because you are on the road alone, you are starved and desperate for sex of any kind. This is a guy who watches way too many dirty movies. However, you are forced to just smile and change the subject, after all, he is a client. This sort of restraint is not necessarily one of my strengths. I can only imagine the sort of looks that cross my face as I gamely try not to say precisely what is on my mind. My father used to say to me, "Darlin', your eyes are meant to be the mirror of your soul, not your entire face."

Traveling for your job is not relaxing in the least, it is grueling. You are always running for a cab, late for a plane, looking for your ticket, or trying to convince the manager of your hotel that, with your confirmation number they have guaranteed you a room. American Express says so. There isn't a whole lot you can say when he looks you in the eye and says, "Yes, I am very sorry but, we don't have any rooms. Not even a closet."

"A closet? When did anyone start talking about me sleeping in a closet?", you want to scream at him but, you are well aware that your greatest chance of sleeping in a bed that night is tightly coupled with your ability to keep your cool.

These guys are well aware that they are holding all of the high cards and they relish their brief dance with power. Why is it they all look as if they have appeared on the "Hair Club for Men" ads? Am I the only one who has noticed that?

This only happens after eleven o'clock at night, in a city that is new to you. If you are fortunate, the manager will try to call around to a couple of places to see if they have a room. Try not to panic as the names of the places he is calling begin to deteriorate. Once he gets down to any place with "Big Mama's" as part of their name, you'd best sleep with your panty hose on. I have even resorted to wedging a chair under the doorknob. That, by the way, looks a lot easier to do on television than it actually is.

The most recent time this happened to me, I was in Albany, New York and received directions from the reservation person, to the location of their hotel, a well known chain, where I had just made a reservation. When I arrived at the hotel that I had received the directions to, the desk clerk informed me that I did not have a reservation. I showed him my confirmation number and he was kind enough to load it into their system and determined it was at one of their other hotels, clear across the city. He wasn't sure how to get there so, he was again kind enough to call them, get directions and tell them I was on my way.

The directions were horrendous but, after calling the hotel again and stopping a state police car, I managed to find my way to the place. I limped into the lobby at twenty minutes past midnight, only to be told they did not have my room. I assured the woman they did. After all, it was I their other location desk clerk had phoned about, letting them know I was on my way and, it was I who had called again, in an attempt to clarify the rotten directions she had provided. I had made it, despite all of the roadblocks they had thrown in my path. No, I assured her, they certainly had a room for me. After all, I am a member of their mega-frequent-tiptop-guest program and they are always sending me mail, telling me how important I am to their organization.

She was carefully examining her six inch long purple fingernails, each with an elaborate design, several with what appeared to be semi-precious jewels glued on to them, as she sighed and said, "Yeah, well sure, he called. But we just rented the room to someone else."

I could not believe what I was hearing so, I asked her to repeat what she had just told me, somewhat shrilly I suspect. Calmly, but without taking her eyes off of her fingernails (if that is even what these works of art would be called) she told me that she had just rented the room to "some guy who just came in."

It is situations such as this which clearly explain why I am adamantly opposed to any individual, not in law enforcement, being permitted to carry around a concealed, loaded weapon. I don't care what Charlton Heston says. We all have our limits and I can tell you quite honestly, I had been pushed well beyond mine. As it was, even without a weapon, utter pandemonium ensued as I became completely unglued, right there in the front office, in front of two women who could not have been less interested in me or where I spent what was left of the night. As near as I could tell, their fingernails were the only thing either one of them had been even remotely interested in, for the previous six or seven years.

I am not so self-involved that I think this is something new or that it only happens to me. No, I realized that this is not a new phenomenon – in fact it is a well documented part of 2,000 years of history. After all, Christ was born in a barn because they rented out their rooms, probably to a higher bidder. That part of the story never made it into any of the songs. I guess that's because it's difficult to find anything that rhymes with "payola".

When I am on the road, the level of intensity really ramps up if I am driving in a part of the country that is unfamiliar to me. That would be any part of the country other than Boston. This is because, whenever this happens, I spend at least half of the time lost on strange roads, with nothing for miles and miles around me and the gas gauge perilously hovering around "E". I then start wondering if my rental has one of those little warning lights or, if I will suddenly find myself walking along in search of a gas station in the middle of nowhere, in the pitch black, wondering exactly why it was I went to graduate school. In these situations, I always talk to myself out loud.

Then, eureka, a gas station appears out of the dark just like in the cartoons when a palm tree appears in the desert. I find that I am both shocked at my unbelievably good fortune and grateful to the god of all road warriors, believing that, once again, I have been saved. I am convinced that this miracle is nothing less than a reward for such clean living. Not only will I be able to fill up my rental car with gasoline but I will also be able to get directions to my next destination. My elation is short lived when I realize it is a self serve gas station and the guys in the little office who were going to set me on a corrected route look like they are out on a work-release program for violent offenders. In fact, the prison might not even be certain of their exact whereabouts.

I am going to give you a little advice here. If you are ever in a strange city or part of the world, driving a rental car, always have a full tank of gas and, whenever possible, buy one of those little maps of the area. I don't care if you can expense it or not – it's short money – more than likely the best five bucks you will ever spend. You really have to trust me on this. Even if you don't believe one other thing I am telling you, this is advice that you should just accept, rather than learn it on your own.

I know what you are thinking but, another universal force that I have uncovered and have yet to mention is that, whenever you are lost or running extremely late for a meeting, you will never be able to get a signal on your cell phone. It must have something to do with the aura caused by the negative energy you are emanating. This stressed out aura must have some sort of cosmic collision with your phone signal, detouring it to somewhere in Detroit. That is, unless you are in Detroit and, in that case, it would end up in Boulder.

Although I do not have specific empirical evidence of this (all of the communication companies are stone walling me) I can confidently state that it happens with such alarming frequency, there must be a scientific explanation. In any event, buy a map and get familiar with it before you start driving. You will be ever so thankful that you did.

By the way, you can never count on directions that you have received from your client, as well meaning as they may be. It is never done with malice but, they always assume you have lived your entire life on the streets they are telling you about, not that it is your first visit to this area of the country. Unfortunately, this assumption always negatively impacts their directions.

I must admit here that I hail from the "Land of Horrendous Directions", Boston. Having traveled around the world, I am willing to step forward and say that Bostonians give the worst directions anywhere.

Again, there is no malice in this, it is just that many of us have never gotten out of town and just assume that everyone knows where "the artery" is. This is assumed, even though "the artery" has never appeared on a map nor is there, to my knowledge, any sign anywhere which would identify this section of roadway as such.

You can stop someone and ask them for directions and, after they have determined what you think about the Bruins or the Red Sox, depending on the time of year they might say something like: "The best way to get there from here would be to make a right onto Newbury Street and go five blocks and make a left. But, you can't do that because it is a one way street."

They then stop talking, give you a great smile and walk away, expecting you to extrapolate from there. It is even worst if you ask a relative of mine, who is not only a Bostonian but Irish as well. Then the directions go something like, "Go past St. Brendan's – the parish, not the convent – then go, oh, I don't know, six or ten blocks until you get to the conner where St. Ann's school used to be."

When you press them for more details, telling them you don't know where anything is now much less where things used to be, and ask them what is there now, they furrow up their brow and tell you they aren't sure what is there now but, their cousin, Michael, got kicked out of St. Ann's for pulling a false alarm in 1964 and no one from the family was ever allowed to attend the school after that.

You are trying to appreciate this little piece of local history and remain calm. Slowly, with a smile on your face, you ask again if he has any idea what might be on that particular corner now. As your guy takes off his Red Sox cap and scratches his head or his belly, giving the appearance of great concentration, a voice from no where shouts out of the bar you are standing in front of, "Yesus Tim, that's where Paddy Clark's brother-in-law – you know, the lad that married Paddy's sister with the red hair – has his pub. I think it's called Harrigan's. No, no, I think that it's called Rosie's. That's it, it's called Rosie's. Take a left there."

It isn't until you get back into your car and begin to drive away that you realize you still have no idea how to get to your client's office.

Is the value of a map becoming apparent to you yet? It is also not a bad investment if you plan to travel by taxi, especially in New York City or Washington, D.C. You jump in a cab in either of these cities and the cabbie immediately asks you how you want to get into the city. You can't fake it by replying, "The best way.", or "Just take the fastest route." You have to sound confident and as if you have some sort of an idea of how to get there and make a suggestion as to the best route. If not, they immediately identify you as a hay seed and you end up with a sixty dollar fare. Study the map when you are still in the airport, if he catches you looking at it in the cab, you're dead.

If your road trip requires that you spend the night in a hotel, things just deteriorate further. Due to the fact you were packing at four o'clock in the morning when it was still pitch black and, God forbid, you turn on a light and wake the king, you find that you have packed one blue and one black shoe. The situation worsens as you proceed to put your thumb through all four of the brand new pairs of panty hose you brought along and, as you take your suit from the dry cleaner's plastic bag, you realized that they didn't get the huge stain off of your jacket. If you're lucky, the skirt will be there and your blouse won't be missing any crucial buttons. This is when you have managed to pack well.

Once you have gotten dressed, you are afraid to eat anything for fear you will end up looking like you had just been in a food fight, when you arrive at your client's office. You can only hope that your stomach won't growl too loudly.

To debunk another myth, if you spent the previous night in a hotel, you have not had a "night out of Dodge"; meaning a little respite for you, some contemplative time alone. Nope, more than likely were on the phone, listening to everything that went wrong in children's day, all because you were not there or helping them with their homework. (Generally I find it to be a combination of both.) My kids knew how to use a fax machine when they were in kindergarten. All of your friends think that you slip out of town, go to the theater or to a very fancy restaurant for a gourmet dinner, perhaps grab a massage, manicure or pedicure – perhaps all three, when you are on the road. The reality is, you are holding vocabulary, geography, history and English quizzes by phone and fax and trying to remember how to simultaneously solve quadratic equations, while you are eating the cup of warm yogurt you grabbed while running through the airport that morning, more than likely, with a cracked plastic spoon. It's similar to childbirth. Until someone experiences it, they can never fully appreciate it, regardless of how many programs they watch on the Discovery channel.

Can you imagine how difficult it is to describe, over the phone, to a ten year old, how to lay out a map of the world, on a blank piece of paper, using only longitude and latitude? Unless you have tried, there is no way you could imagine the challenge. And of course, as he grows more and more frustrated with your inability to help, he screams at you, "I just don't understand why you can't be here."

The next morning, ridden with guilt, and once again getting a lousy night's sleep, you try to go into your client meeting appearing fresh and focused. This gets a little derailed when you pull the manila folder from your brief case, thinking you will be handing out copies of your client's portfolio, only to find this folder filled with the vocabulary worksheets and math tests you had been administering the previous evening. Thank god for fax machines. And Prozac.

When I was in school, if your parents helped you at all with your homework, you received a failing grade. It was considered cheating. Now, the entire curriculum from kindergarten through high school is built around the assumption that not only do all of the parents have PhD's, but also, none of them have a job or anything else that might distract them from the family's homework assignments. I have been hundreds of miles away from home and have had a hysterical child on the telephone, many more times than once, proclaiming that my career is obviously much more important to me that his education. It has always been clear to my children that they are the only people in their class, perhaps the entire country, with a mother who is not fully committed to both their education as well as their athletic careers. I suppose I should be thankful they never took up a musical instrument.

You are probably wondering why my children were left with only me as a source for their homework help. Their father was also at work so he was not available. However, our children were not latch key children, those who have to go home to an empty house after school. Hardly. We paid a small fortune to have a series of live-in nannies to care for them. This was the only solution we could find, given the long hours we both worked and the unpredictable travel schedule we both had. The nanny's duties did not extend to home-work for many reasons, the primary one being that most of them barely spoke English. It was frightening enough having them behind the wheel of our car, driving our children from event to event.

At this point I would be less than truthful if I did not mention one of my aces-in-the-holes in the homework department. Although I am not lucky enough to have any sisters of my own, my husband has three as well as two sisters-in-law and together, we are six sisters. This is so wonderful for me because they are not only sisters but very close friends, always willing to drop everything and help any time they can.

Aunt Miffy, is now the principal of an elementary school in a contiguous town however, before her elevation to "Queen-of-the-School", she taught math for many years. She is an extremely skilled teacher, able to instruct the most complex math theory, over the telephone. If she feels that it is not being clearly understood, she jumps in her car and arrives for a one-on-one. She is very patient and always has the time for her nephews, despite the many demands on her personal and professional life. Just knowing that she is there for them when I am away from home, gives me tremendous peace of mind. That goes for all of the sisters. I can't tell you how many frantic calls I have made from airports, realizing no one would be there for the ride to the hockey game, pickup dinner or any number of things. They happily take the children overnight and, because they have done it so many times, my children are very comfortable in their homes. "The Sisters" could well be one of the factors that have allowed me to cling to whatever sanity I have left, when I am on the road. Forget those Master Card ads; they are priceless.

As any parent will passionately attest, the child care situation in the United States is deplorable. Anyone who has small children and works outside the home can tell you about it, regardless of their socio-economic bracket. After exhausting every local resource and contact we had, we used an organization that could legally bring a young lady from overseas into the country on a cultural exchange visa. For a fee of many thousands of dollars they would check references and arrange for a legal visa and the nanny would supposedly stay for 13 months. I think the only thing they checked was if she had a pulse and the 13 months – what a joke.

The nanny stories could be a book of their own but, unless you have lived through it yourself, you will think most of them are made up. I must begin by stating that we had some wonderful nannies, thankfully, who were truly a part of our family. We loved them, our children loved them and there were many tears when it was time for them to leave. One of our favorites even came back with her new husband on their honeymoon and stayed with us for two weeks while they traveled around the area. We loved him too. These were the exceptions.

The agency that brings the nannies into the country has coordinators in each area that meet regularly with the girls, with the idea to help them with the transition, meet the other nannies and give them advice on how to deal with any situation or problem that arise as a result of living with a new family.

The girls would meet at least monthly and discuss their particular situations. In a small town such as ours, the nannies all knew each other and we knew most of the families that they lived with. Talk about an invasion of privacy – wow! You'd be at the fish market on a Saturday afternoon and one of your friends would come in laughing and loudly announce she heard that you and your husband had a knock-down drag out argument the previous evening over whether or not you paid too much for your new living room drapes. It's enough to make you take a close look at who your friends really are. That took some real getting used to.

You go from being the parents of a baby to having an 18 year old blabbermouth living in your house. You consider this person an employee and they consider themselves an international guest who has come to party. They stay out until all hours of the night and feel that a hang over is a legitimate excuse for not having to work that day. This, of course, is not the conversation you want to be having at 6:30

on a Wednesday morning. Personally, I find that my persuasive powers don't really kick in until about 10 or 11 AM.

One of the coordinators informed us, somewhat tentatively, that our nanny was telling all of the other nannies in their monthly meetings how we forced her to take our children out of the house all weekend so we could have wild sex, all over the house. Didn't I wish that was the case! Fortunately for us and perhaps unfortunately for me, everyone in town was aware that my husband spends the entire weekend on the golf course so, they dismissed her prattling as malicious gossip, although it could have seriously enhanced my reputation among all of the other mothers, had it been true. This same nanny took a vacation to Hawaii and decided to stay there. We were not sad to hear that she was leaving our family, but we were frantic that we were left without child-care. Despite the fact she had stolen from us, lied to us and about us, she still didn't look as bad as the "next unknown".

We had some small measure of comfort, although it turned out to be totally misguided and short lived. You see, part of the astronomical agency fee is a guarantee that they will replace a nanny who washes out on you before the thirteen months is up, which she most surely did. That fact was not in dispute. What they don't make clear upfront is, if they come up with a warm body, that's who you get. Like it or lump it. So consequently, they replaced the liar with a sociopath. I am not kidding.

We were given a nanny who had been with a family in Colorado. The agency would not let us talk with the family because they didn't want us to have any preconceived negative assumptions about her. Now, why wasn't that an enormous red flag? It has to do with the level of desperation you feel around childcare.

Things did not start out well and our dreadful beginning should have been an indicator of things to come but, we were desperately in need of child care so, we sucked it up and attempted to make it work. She was a very angry young woman, who was always in an incredibly bad mood, that she had no problem letting everyone all around her know about. She had a pissed off look on her face that could stop Arnold in his tracks. Plus, she was French so, whenever she didn't feel like talking or listening, she would just throw up the language barrier and pretend she could not understand what I was saying. Not exactly the type of person you want taking care of your young children. We were trying to figure out how much we should or could put up with when things took a really bad turn.

I was standing in the kitchen one morning, emptying the dishwasher and I noticed that my huge carving knife was not in the block with all of the other knives. Because we only use this during the holidays or if we have a really big barbeque, it was immediately apparent. I couldn't figure out where it possibly could have gone so, I turned to our nanny and asked her if she had any idea of where it could be. She said yes, it was in her room. When I asked why, she informed me that she had been sleeping with it. I am not exaggerating when I tell you that my knees got weak and I felt slightly dizzy. Despite this, I managed to remain outwardly cool and asked her why. I asked if she was fearful of anyone in our family, the neighbors, anyone at all. She said no, that it just made her feel better to have it.

Inside, I was freaking out, outwardly I attempted a very measured affect. I told her that it was not acceptable and that she must replace it, which she reluctantly did. However, the next day it was gone again and she admitted that it was back in her room. I called the coordinator and said that she had to be out of my house in one hour. I didn't care where she went but, she could not stay with us. The coordinator wanted to put her on some sort of a two week trial deal but we were adamant, she had to go.

As a result of several different circumstances, to get her out of my house that day, I ended up taking her to the airport. Suddenly, the agency did not want the responsibility of having her in the country, much less at my house, and got her a ticket back to France. This was prior to Louise Woodward.

After unloading her bags at the airport, I turned to say goodbye and wish her good luck. All I wanted was to have her as far away from my family as possible. I guess she must have felt the same way because, as I turned to speak to her, she slugged me. Yup, right there are Logan Airport; investment professional and French nanny in a fist fight. What a headline. Fortunately it didn't come to that. Actually it wasn't a fight at all because I didn't swing back. Before you decide that I am a wimp, I should add that, at the time, I was five months pregnant.

I wish this sort of a nanny nightmare was unique but, there are thousands of similar stories. One of my friends is a doctor, as is her husband, and they have three children. Like all of us, they are extremely dependent upon their child care provider. So dependent that, even though their nanny stole their car in the middle of the night, disappeared for ten days, leaving only a note that said, "I am sorry" they didn't fire her when she came back. She was too good with the children to risk it. After the grand theft auto, she got pregnant while she was living with them and she and her baby lived with them for quite a while. In fact, they stayed there until her mother arrived and brought the baby back to Jamaica. Despite the fact they had been working around all of the issues incumbent with her having an infant, one that was not in the original hiring discussion, they were so happy that she didn't go back to Jamaica with them, they gave her a raise.

Why are we always finding ourselves in situations where we are asking ourselves, "Who is really in charge here?" We thought that once we conquered the Fat White Boys, we'd be done. It would be over and we would be staring eye to eye with everyone, based on merit. Little did we know that, until our children could drive, we would end up total dependant on someone else who could.

Not everyone hears the words "nanny" or "child care" and cringes. Generally the words have a much greater negative effect upon mothers. To my point, my husband and his friends would greatly anticipate the huge summer influx of the "Euro-Nannies" as they call them because these girls, being a little less uptight than their American counterparts, loved to sunbath topless around the pool at our club. These men practically had a hole on the golf course moved so they would have more reasons to continue to walk by the pool, again and again. This was before a few of the wives banded together to insure that this sunbathing practice would not, under any circumstances, be tolerated.

As much as I can honestly say that I could not have cared

less about the topless sunbathing, there is something completely unnatural about having a gorgeous young thing living in your home, directly after you have given birth. You are more hormonal than at any other point in your life and your body is not your own. This should be a very private time, not one that is witnessed by a complete stranger.

Another one of my friends is very funny when she talks about going to the airport, six weeks after giving birth, still feeling about as sexy as Margaret Thatcher, to meet her family's new nanny. She knew that the girl was from Sweden but, she was still thoroughly unprepared to see "six foot long legs, topped by lots and lots of blonde hair" walking toward her. She said that she closed her eyes and shot off the quick, "Oh please God, don't let that be her." only to see the arms attached to these long legs waving happily, as she recognized her name on the sign my friend was holding. She briefly contemplated running out of the airport without her and telling her husband, "I don't know why she didn't come. She must have changed her mind." You want to talk about motivation to lose that extra weight you put on? There is nothing else quite so compelling – if only we could bottle it. Step aside Weight Watchers.

Not only is this sweet young thing living in your house, but if you travel, she is living in your house, with your husband, without you. That's a lot to think about. Especially if your husband starts making subtle little suggestions such as, it might be really relaxing for you if you stay an extra day on the West Coast and see the sights. This is the same guy who would turn purple at the mere thought of you being out of town and leaving him with the children for an evening.

The good thing is, by virtue of having children, you have your own personal network of spies so, not too much can go on without their knowing about it. If they are too small to talk, have one of your good friends drop in at odd times of the day, "just to see if anyone needs any help". Have her do it often enough to keep everyone on their toes and to send a clear message that you might be out of town but you are not out of sight. It's all manageable, sometimes it just involves developing new skills sets.

Another thing that I have observed is, to be able to survive and remain sane in this sort of an environment; you not only get very creative but also quite adept at arranging things on the phone. Long before the Internet, I became quite skilled at catalogue shopping, often doing 90% of my Christmas shopping at 11 o'clock at night, with a glass of wine and my VISA. I would have a list of everyone I was purchasing a gift for, the catalogue it was coming from and, of course, what the item was. By 1 AM, my list would also include the order number(s) and the expected ship date for each gift. As the gifts came in, I would check them against the master list, wrap them and stick them in a pile in my guest room. There were many years that I completed all of my holiday shopping without ever entering a mall.

Because I really dislike shopping, a fact most of my friends can not even begin to process, I have always bought most of my clothes from catalogues. My children will come into the living room and I'll be sitting there with a glass of wine, a stack of catalogues and the phone and they will say, "Oh Mum, are you shopping?" I am pretty sure that they don't realize that most mothers go to stores to buy things.

The only down side that I have been able to discern from this is that catalogues are like rabbits, they breed at an astonishing rate. Once you order from one, they sell your name to every other catalogue that has ever been published and for some inexplicable reason, I find myself feeling obligated to look through each one that has been delivered to my house.

This is cause for some hostility within my household because I tend to leave stacks of them all over the house, with little stickies, marking the pages I want to look at again, to consider a purchase. My husband is not a catalogue shopper and he does not understand my need to look carefully at each one that comes into our home. He refers to them collectively and quite derisively as "Your Magazines" and is always threatening to throw them all out. He never does though, because he knows that he may just throw away one in which I have marked off a gift for him.

I have negotiated many things over the phone, completed a lot of commerce and made arrangements for more things than I can tell you. Last summer, my husband and I hosted a cocktail party on a schooner that was berthed in a nearby harbor. We bid on this at an auction we attended, thinking it would be a lot of fun for a summer party. That was on a very cold evening in November when, the logistics of arranging a party in another town were not anything I even considered. However, with a phone and a fax I was confident that it would all go off quite smoothly.

I had met with the caterer and planned the menu and bar service. We also had a photographer, which I had arranged over the phone. I was then discussing the logistics of the evening, as far as the layout of the tables and chairs, with the person in charge of the schooner. I was under the impression things moving along quite smoothly until she said, sounding somewhat put out, "Well, when are you going to come down here?"

I assured her I would be there before the guests arrived and that our caterer was quite familiar with the layout of the schooner. There was a long pause, causing me to finally ask, "Is that alright?"

She then said, sounding quite pained, "Well, yes, I guess so. We have just never had anyone plan a party here, never having seen it first. Are you absolutely sure you don't want to come down here before your party?" Her tone of voice indicated that not only was I insulting her as well as the schooner, it was clear to her that she was dealing with some-one who had no concept whatsoever of all that is involved in throwing a party. Little did she know she was talking to the "Queen of Arrangements by Telephone".

How could I tell her, the invitations were in the mail, the caterer would be there and, at this point, me seeing things could only highlight potential problems? Problems I did not have time to resolve. No, I assured her, everything sounded fine and I was quite comfortable seeing it all on the evening of the party. In fact, I was looking forward to it.

I didn't think I should tell her about purchasing my son's Jeep over the phone. One of my sister-in-laws told me this was my ultimate coup of catalogue shopping. I'll let you decide if you agree.

Our older son was driving one of our old, old cars. It was

twelve years old, with 260,000 miles on it, and it was sorely in need of a major overhaul. I don't need to tell you why the idea of dumping five or six thousand dollars into this junk was not attractive, not to mention the fact he is going to school in Vermont and this particular car is like a sled in the snow. My husband was in Scotland (Guess what? He was playing golf.). I was working and not able to take any time off to go car shopping. The immediate problem was that our son needed a car to go to work and school and the junk was finally on its very last legs. Once again, there was no down time and no wiggle room.

What to do? In my younger years, I will admit to you that this may have stumped me but, after all of these years of "cut and paste", I have gotten quite resourceful. My father was fond of saying, "The only obstacles before us are those we have placed there ourselves." I don't know if Disraeli or perhaps Winston Churchill who said it first, but I grew up hearing him say it and I grew to believe it.

So, what to do? I called my brother-in-law, and asked him for the telephone number of a car dealer we have all used in the past. My brother-in-law is a current, good customer of this dealership and he is the type of guy everyone knows and loves. You always get a great response whenever you drop his name anywhere. That is, after the people stop laughing about something he either said or did. He is a very funny guy but, there is no one more helpful when you are in a jam. If he can't personally help you out himself, he knows at least six people who can.

This particular car dealership sells Mercedes and BMWs, neither of which we had any intention of purchasing for this child. I was looking for some sort of a four wheel drive vehicle that would not go too fast and would be safe in the snow. I was wishing that the military sold their old tanks. But, as luck would have it, my brother-in-law happened to know that a Jeep had been traded in the previous day, on a new Mercedes purchase. He knew this because he had sent the customer to the dealership. This would only surprise someone who did not know my brother-in-law.

The fact that my son was in Vermont, the car dealership was in New Hampshire and I was in Massachusetts, about to leave for New York, was not anything I was going to let get in my way. Especially since things were starting to come together.

The fabulous Crystal, the manager of pre-owed vehicles from the dealership, called me because my brother-in-law had called her to tell her he had sold the Jeep for her. (Because she knows him quite well, I doubt very much she was surprised that one of her customers, who had never worked at a car dealership, had just sold a car for her; a used car that had been on the lot fewer than twenty-four hours.)

We agreed on a price and Crystal agreed to accept a personal check from me on delivery. But, before the Jeep could be delivered, I had to get it registered and insured. To accomplish this I had to work between three states so, it was a little tricky especially because I could not leave my office.

Our Massachusetts insurer could not insure our son in Vermont. They did not have a relationship with an insurer in Vermont and no suggestions on how to find one that would be willing to transact business with a total stranger over the phone. Because we are talking about insurance, I might also mention that my son is not what could be classified as a "good insurance risk". That is actually an extraordinary understatement.

I called one of my clients in Vermont and explained my dilemma. He volunteered to call his insurance agent, explain the entire situation, including my son's not so stellar driving record, and see if they would accept him as a client. Miraculously, they said yes, based on the long standing relationship they have had with my client. I sent them a check by overnight mail and they supplied an insurance binder for the Jeep.

I called my son and told him to get home immediately with the junk because, I had even managed to get a trade-in as part of this whole deal. Now, it really gets beautiful.

One of the salesmen at the (New Hampshire) dealership had to attend a funeral in Massachusetts so, he agreed to deliver the Jeep to my house, pick up the old car, attend the funeral and deliver the old car back to New Hampshire. Because I had to leave for New York, I left a check taped to my front door, with a thank you note, mentioning my sincere hope that it didn't rain, due to the fact that not only was the front window on the driver's side punched out but also, the windshield wipers didn't work.

All of this without leaving my office. Sometimes, it's just knowing who to call. And don't try calling me, asking for my brother-in-law's number, because I will not part with it.

Is all this worth it? The answer to that question changes every day. I have always worked and have always wanted to work, at least theoretically; however there have been many days when I would have given nearly anything I had, if I could have just stayed home. Each of us has many very good, well thought out reasons why we have chosen what we have; we just have to remember them, or remind each other, on the bad days.

One thing though, that I hope may be helpful, is the following compilation of suggestions or tips, many of which I am sure appear to be simple common sense, to aid those of us who attempt to have a family and work at a job where we have to travel. This makes us **Road Warriors** and soldiers always stick together. This is a powerful and unique sister-hood.

As I have said so many times while writing this book, these suggestions or tips, could be a stand-alone book and they are certainly not exhaustive. I am going to try to consolidate the list to what I believe to be the absolute essentials. These were all learned by me or by one of more of my good friends, the hard way. Don't be like our children and refuse to accept the benefit of our experiences without having to go ahead and experience it for yourself. I mean, how many of us have to be in Houston, Texas, in what was then a Shearson Lehman office, with our hand stuck in a tampon machine? Really, isn't one of us enough? Such an absolutely humiliating event should be a group learning experience. Just be very grateful we are willing to share. Of course, I invite you to add to the list – I am always willing to learn, even eager, if I can do so without incurring yet another colossal humiliation. At this late stage in my life, I am ready for dignity.

Tips From an Old Road Warrior

"If we're treading on thin ice, we might as well dance."
-Jesse Winchester

There are some simple necessities that you should have with you whenever you leave the house. Once you go on the road they become even more crucial because, when you are in a strange city, pressed for time, you don't want to be wandering around, looking for a pharmacy or some such thing. It will only add to your stress level and our number one goal when on the road should be:

Above All, Remain Calm

Ralph Waldo Emerson is famous for, among other things, his *Essays on Self Reliance*. Although I am, by no means insinuating that I have anywhere near the gift for writing that Emerson did, I do hope you find the following equally helpful and perhaps even a bit more current.

ITEMS YOU MUST CARRY WITH YOU AT ALL TIMES:

1. Always have a mending kit, with buttons and every color thread imaginable. It is always the hot pink thread that you need, never the navy blue.

2. It is impossible to have too many pairs of panty hose with you.

3. Bring your own hair products because unless you are in a really swanky hotel, the stuff they supply is really cheap. Plus, if you need corrective eye wear to be able to read anything, especially early in the morning, you could find yourself in the pickle of putting what you thought to be conditioner into your hair and finding out it was body lotion.

Author's Note: There are only two ways to get body lotion out of your hair; shave your head completely and wait for the new hair to grow in or use lighter fluid.

There is much to be said for having hair products in bottles that are easily recognizable.

4. Not only should you always have a box of tampons in your desk and few spares in your briefcase, you should never leave home without a fist full of them in your overnight bag and your carryon luggage.

The first time you do, regardless of how "regular" you are, you will find yourself in dire need. Trust me, it's another force of nature I have uncovered. How would you have liked to have been the person that the flight attendant had to make the request for, over the plane's PA system on a Boston – LA flight? I realize that is a rhetorical question but, I pose it only to make my point. You can sit there, telling yourself you will never see any of these people again but, you will still find yourself shrinking to almost nothing, as the flight attendant walks toward you with the tampon.

Each time you go on the road, your primary objective before you leave your house should be to minimize any sort of jam you could find yourself in. This is a small precaution to take toward that objective and believe me, you will get down on your knees overcome by gratitude and thank me for making you realize the importance of this very thing, the first time you find yourself in this particular sort of need.

5. Always have plenty of your pain killer of choice. Traveling creates an insidious form of stress which is always lurking in

the quasi-background, ready to explode into a headache of gargantuan proportion, given the slightest provocation. The provocations are without end and combined with the food-on-the-run diet of a road warrior, I always am in some stage of a headache. Because of this, I always travel with the Advil 500 capsule container and pop them as if they were M&Ms.

If you suffer from allergies, do not leave town without plenty of Benadryl. There is little worse than being covered from head to toe with hives when you are in a strange city, barely able to breathe. The concierge is never quite sure what to make of you.

6. Pack a small battery operated alarm clock. It has been well documented that you can only trust the hotel desk to accurately make your wake up call 50% of the time. The likelihood of them getting it right is inversely related to how important your first morning meeting is and how much you had to drink the night before.

7. Always have a good book with you. When on the road you can be stuck in any place imaginable place and some places where you will spend the rest of your life hoping you never have to imagine again. When you are in this sort of situation, it is never fun but, at least if you have a book you have something with which to occupy yourself. Otherwise you find yourself playing some sort of solo version of the *Gong Show* as you are people watching, wondering exactly where these people go when they are not hanging around an airport. Perhaps a bus station?

8. Always pack a razor. Because although you will not be going out for a gourmet dinner or attending a Broadway

opening, you will have ten or fifteen minutes, all to yourself, where you can actually get into the bathtub alone and shave your legs without being interrupted. This is a luxury and the only time I am ever able to shave my legs without looking as if I have been in some sort of religious ceremony that has involved blood letting.

9. I am not a proponent of over packing but, if you can fit them in, it is always great to have a pair of sneakers with you. They come in so handy if you need to run through the airport, or anywhere else for that matter. Even if you don't want to work out, sometimes just being able to take a brisk walk outside after working all day can really freshen you up. And, if you have had a long day and your dogs are barking, it feels so good to slip into your sneaks. It's almost as good as sex.

10. It can never hurt to have a roll of duct tape with you.

If you travel frequently, which to me is more than twice a month, I recommend packing a bag with duplicates all of the bathroom/cosmetic stuff you use. That way, you only have to remember to replace what you have run out of, rather than repack the same bag each week. It is a fabulous time saving measure and one you will be very happy you have undertaken, when you realize that to make your plane, you should have left your house fifteen minutes ago and you are still in your underwear.

Nearly everyone I know who travels frequently would agree with the above statement. The area of debate – each with a compelling argument – is whether to pack those little bitty bottles that you have to fill, or go with the larger size that you use at home. The little bottles are great if you are extremely focused on lightening your load. I find that they are always empty even though it seems that I had just filled them the previous week. Plus squirting cream rinse into a little bottle is really messy. This is a matter of personal preference and for you to decide yourself.

HOTEL TIPS:

1. If, when you are checking in to the hotel, the meathead behind the desk yells out your name and room number to a bellhop, as in, "Hey Whitey, will you bring Mimi O'Bara's bags up to room 756?", quietly, but firmly, demand another room.

There are creeps that hang out in lobbies just hoping for this kind of information, and then they stalk you. Some call your room from a house phone, as they have your name and room number and harass you. Some even come and knock on your door. Don't risk it, get another room. Most places are very hip to this and they won't make a fuss. If they do, it's your turn to make a fuss.

2. Don't feel as if you have to eat in your room because you don't want to look stupid eating alone in the hotel restaurant. You are not stupid, you are a Warrior and as such have worked up a mighty powerful appetite. When I first began to travel for work, it was always a cold steak sandwich and a limp salad consisting of wilted iceberg lettuce and tomatoes that could be used in major league baseball game, eaten in my room. Sometimes that is fine but usually you are so hungry you want real food, or at least something luke warm.

Back then, people also made unkind assumptions about you. Approximately fifteen years ago I was sitting in the lobby of a very highly regarded hotel in Denver. I was wearing a navy blue business suit, reading the Wall Street Journal, waiting for a colleague I was meeting for dinner. A man approached me and began to ask me rather peculiar questions, in an odd attempt to start of conversation. It took me a couple of minutes to realize that he thought I was a hooker. I don't even wear make-up.

This left me absolutely stunned. After sharing the story with a few of my friends who also traveled rather regularly for their work and expecting them to be as shocked and outraged as I, I was stunned again to find that this was not an isolated event. They had each had it happen to them on several occasions, in several different cities. I am fairly certain that such a thing would not happen now.

Most hotels these days are aware that women travel alone and they are very accommodating. They realize they have to be or we will spread the word and business women will no longer go to their hotels and restaurants. In the old days, if you were so bold as to go into a restaurant without an escort, they would make you wait forever and then reluctantly give you a table that was practically in the kitchen. For the most part, those days are over.

If some well meaning person insists that you join them for dinner, only do so if you want to. Don't be bullied into eating with someone you don't know, just because they are standing there insisting. Those people always creep me out.

When I go into a restaurant by myself, I bring a book, ask for a table that is well lit and talk only to the wait staff. If some guy comes over thinking he is going to do me a big favor by having dinner with me, I politely say "no thanks", without even taking my face out of the book. A nice guy understands immediately that you are not interested and leaves you alone. A creep continues to badger you and, with a creep, all bets are off. You can be as rude as you would like. Just make sure that he doesn't follow you out to your car. If you think that he might be lurking outside, don't hesitate to ask the manager to walk to your car with you. They will happily do that for you at any decent restaurant. Don't be shy.

I find myself in Albany, New York quite frequently on business and I often eat at The Outback Restaurant because not only is their food really good but also because of how aware the entire staff is of this sort of situation. They are warm and welcoming each time I come in by myself and, if there is ever an occasion where someone is bothering me, the staff is so well trained and hip that it is handled in a smooth and professional manner, where no one is made to feel uncomfortable. Most of the staff is not much older than my oldest son and I am certain that they believe that my days of being a love goddess are long gone yet; they are always aware and responsive of what is going on, without being intrusive. They must have a very good training program.

3. While we are on the topic of food – try to eat sensibly – or at least as sensibly as you do at home. It is so easy to grab 3,600 calories of junk food when you are galloping across the country. Unfortunately, stress does not burn calories, only brain cells.

Believe me, I know how easy and tempting it is, when you are racing through an airport, absolutely famished, to grab two candy bars and a bag of chips. You know it's not the right thing to do but, after all, you have earned it. Not only is this a guarantee for a sugar headache, you will be just as hungry in about 90 minutes. After six months of this, unless it is the way your always eat, you will have added two sizes onto your butt and thighs, which is not a good thing.

It is just as easy to carry a couple pieces of fruit and some bottled water with you. Not only will you feel so much better, you will only be replacing your wardrobe every season, because you want to.

4. If you are given a room either next to or across from the elevator or ice machine, get another room. Unless the hotel is completely sold out, don't take no for an answer, if it is your intention to get any sleep at all.

The elevator pings and dings all night long as the doors bang open and crash close, not to mention the long involved conversations drunk people feel obligated to have, on the top of their lungs, as they are getting off of the elevator together, right in front of your door, at 2 AM. Why is it that all drunks think they are great singers?

And, there is nothing quite like the sound of someone digging one of those large plastic scoops into the ice machine about 3AM. The only possible reason anyone would want ice at 3 AM is related to alcohol. They have usually had way too much and are hoping to continue to have still more. This makes their ice gathering process seventeen times louder and six times longer than that of a sober person at 7 PM.

Many years ago, I was in a hotel room in Atlanta, Georgia one night, directly across from the ice machine. At this point in my young career, I did not realize how hazardous this particular room location was. But, I was soon to be enlightened.

I was in all tucked into bed and happily reading a Stephen King novel. Right when I got to a particularly hair raising part, where I was holding my breath and absolutely terrified, someone dug into the ice machine across the hall, making such a sound that I damn near had a heart attack. I do not remember sailing out of my bed, screaming, or tearing my book in half. All I can tell you is that I found myself across the room, shaking all over, with my book in two pieces, in two different parts of the room, realizing that someone in the room had screamed very loudly. I am surprised that no one called 911. This is not an experience I would ever want to repeat.

LESSONS LEARNED:

1. Never ever get your hair cut or colored in a strange city, no matter how bad it looks or how much free time you have. Just think about it, what are the chances that the hairdresser who is available to take a walk-in is any good at all? If they were, they would be working on one of their regulars and have a six week waiting list.

Once, finding myself with a free afternoon in Denver, I actually ended up with a perm and green hair that was so hideous that even the biggest practical joker in our office did not say a word when he saw me. There are not words that could describe how awful I looked.

Months and months later, when most of the green frizz was gone, I told him that it was only when I saw him and he didn't say a word about it, that I was certain of the extent of the damage. His eyes got really big and he said, "I felt so sorry for you, it looked so bad. I didn't even know you could get hair to do that. I was afraid you might even start crying or something if I mentioned it. Plus, I knew that Charlene (his wife) would have killed me." The memory alone is enough to make me cry, even to this day.

2. Don't bring new shoes with you unless you are not planning on walking anywhere or unless you also bring an old broken in pair. It is amazing how painful and bloody blisters are and, once you have only one, it is impossible to walk with any dignity or air of professionalism.

The day after walking up the hills of San Francisco, in new shoes with two inch heels, I was running through the San Francisco airport in bare feet because I could not put those shoes on and there was no time for me to buy new ones. I had so many bandages on them, I looked as if my feet had been bound in some ancient Asian ceremony. You can only imagine the looks I got when I arrived in Boston. The fact it was snowing out made my choice of foot ware appear even more bizarre. It was just one more time I found myself thinking, "Well hell, it's not like I am going to see any of these people again."

3. Never dive into a wading pool.

4. Don't think that just because you are out of town, you won't see anyone you know or, more to the point, that no one you know will see you. As Maisey used to say, "You can run, Child, but you can't hide." There are many things that can be extrapolated from this particular observation but, what I took away from it was that, no matter how far away I was from her, she would always find out everything that I did. Not only that, the worse the offense, the quicker she would learn about it. And because it did seem to work out that way with a high level of frequency, it served to generally keep me on my toes, at least throughout my high school years.

However, this was never brought home to me with such impact as when a very good friend of mine who was having an affair, met up with her man in a city thousands of miles away from either of their homes. They had a lovely romantic dinner with lots of champagne and then checked into their hotel. Everything was going along quite smoothly until about 3 AM when there was a fire alarm and they had to evacuate. There they were, standing outside in those little hotel bathrobes, obviously naked and together, and who should they spot but someone they both knew, who was very well aware there was no good reason for them to be together, especially dressed in such a manner. Further proving Maisey's point; they also made the local six o'clock news, the following evening. When in doubt, never let "What are chances?" be your swing vote. Listen to your inner voice.

On a lighter note, but making the same point, a very good friend of mine wanted to go down to the Super Bowl with a bunch of his buddies, one year when it was being held in New Orleans. His wife, who is a very sensible woman, said absolutely not. She said that it would just be a four day drunk and that he was far too old for such nonsense.

Well, he was outraged by the suggestion and let her know it. He told her how offended he was that she would think that just because he was at a football game, far away from home, he wouldn't be on his most gentlemanly behavior.

She finally got tired of listening to him whine about it and told him to go ahead but she did not expect him to come home all sick and hung over. Again, shock and outrage were expressed at the very thought she would even suggest such a thing.

Two days later, down in New Orleans, he found himself singing and marching in a parade with all of his buddies, each of whom had a pair of women's panties on their head. (This is a man who, at the time, had three grown children.) They were so drunk that when the photographer from AP asked them where they were from, they proudly shouted out the name of their home town. The very next day, there they were, the local Super Bowl attendees, on the front page of their local paper, as happy as Larry and wearing women's panties on their heads. To the best of my knowledge, this was his last Super Bowl. Now that I think of it, I am not even sure they made it to the game.

5. Be resourceful but not impulsive. By that I mean, think your solutions through before implementation. I remember the time when I was quite a bit younger and still believing that it could all be perfect, all the time. (This is never a safe thought to carry around because you will find yourself in a perpetual state of disappointment.)

I was in a client's office, waiting for him to get his coat so we could go to lunch. As I was standing there, I looked down at my own new winter coat and, much to my horror, I saw that the hem on the lining had torn somehow and was hanging below the coat. This would never do. I was horrified and momentarily paralyzed. Then, I arrived at the perfect solution.

Looking around, making sure no one could see me, with lightening speed, I grabbed the stapler from my client's desk and stapled the lining back up so it was no longer hanging below the coat. I was filled with self congratulations, stunning even myself at my quick response and ingenious remedy. Unfortunately, all this back slapping was short lived.

As we were walking to the restaurant and my coat was swinging back and forth against my stockings, I realized I had not been as quite as resourceful as I had initially believed. In my rush to staple the lining, I did not think about which side of the staple to have brushing against my legs. It should have been the flat side. I did it the other way, effectively putting little saws inside my coat, resulting in my stockings being sliced off at about mid calf.

When I looked down and saw my stockings – to say they were barely hanging on by a thread is a true and accurate description – I thought I would die right there. But then, the absurdity of the situation was too much for me and I burst out laughing. In fact, I was laughing so hard, I could barely explain to my perplexed client exactly what the matter was. Once I showed him, he was laughing so hard, we were in the middle of the sidewalk, howling with laughter, holding one another up. And didn't we get some strange looks from the other pedestrians.

He was a very good client of mine for a long time and, whenever we were both at a very large and important dinner, he would make me retell the story, much to my embarrassment.

6. This tip is from my previously quoted, very good buddy, Lucy, herself a veteran Road Warrior. Never look at yourself in the mirror in the airplane bathroom. Every zit is magnified or they suddenly appear the minute you open the door. You look as if you are in the last stages of liver disease, your skin and the whites of your eyes are so yellow. Bow your head when washing your hands and exit quickly.

This piece of very good advice from Lucy got me thinking about mirrors in general and, perhaps this should be in the "hotel section" but, because it is "mirror advice", I am going to leave it here.

Be very careful when you are in a hotel walking around naked, that you never allow yourself a surprise glimpse of the back of your legs and fanny, unless you are so masochistic that you do this on a regular basis. It is absolutely terrifying to see what time, gravity and no muscle tone have done. If you are walking around nude, don't wear your glasses. It's best that way, after all, there are some things we just don't need to know.

7. Now, I am going to get serious for a quick bit. Listen up.

If you are walking anywhere but especially at night in a strange city, make sure you know exactly where you are going and that your route is well traveled and well lit. Get your directions before you leave your hotel. Walk with confidence, briskly and with your head held up, looking straight ahead. Be aware of your surroundings. And, depending on how you feel about this, you might want to carry pepper spray. You can't carry it on an airplane so, if you need to fly with it, pack it in a checked bag. You can buy it on-line from www.herringtoncatalog.com.

If you ever sense that you are not safe, trust your instincts. It is far preferable to appear to be a wimp than to put yourself into a situation where you are not comfortable. And, quite honestly, it is my experience that our instincts or our inner voice are generally very accurate. Be alert and do not be afraid to ask for help. This is not a situation where you need to prove anything to anyone. You may be a "Warrior" but that doesn't make you invincible.

ON THE ROAD CLIENT INTERACTION:

1. If you are out with a client, never get drunk, regardless of how much your client is drinking. There is no possible good ending to this sort of an evening. Stick to sparkling water.

2. Never talk religion or politics with your client unless you are completely willing to subordinate all of your own personal beliefs and just agree with what they are saying. I find this to be a nearly impossible feat so, I avoid these topics at all costs. Otherwise, I find that the conversation deteriorates into something quite ugly as my views tend to be somewhat liberal.

During the Clarence Thomas confirmation hearings I had to attend all my client meetings with a muzzle on. I brought along a chalk board and just wrote down anything that I had to say with regard to their portfolio.

The difficult thing about conversations of this nature is, there are no right answers but each of us tenaciously hangs onto our beliefs. Jill Conner Browne is absolutely hilarious on this topic in her book, *The Sweet Potato Queens Book of Love* once having had a theological discussion be reduced to the penetrating question, "What if Jesus was a mongoose?" If you have not already done so, I suggest that you read the book if you are curious about how the discussion evolved to this point. She also has a lot of other very useful information, hints and observations that I personally have found to be immensely beneficial as well as entertaining.

3. If you are having dinner with a married male client, always invite his wife to come along. Even if she doesn't attend, you have sent him a clear message. If you know this guy, you know what his intentions are and most are pretty innocuous. But, men being men, even the nicest ones are always looking for an opening. So just be on your toes and be aware at all times that this is a business relationship and nothing more.

And then there are the slime balls but, they can be handled. The following is advice for handing the slime balls. In time, you will develop your own individual methods for handling this sort of a guy but, until then, pay careful attention to these.

After you cover your business topics thoroughly, spend the remainder of your time together talking about his family and your family. If he just stonewalls you on his family, talk about yours. If you don't have a husband, talk about your boyfriend – even if you haven't had a date in five years. Keep it light and don't let him draw you into a conversation about sex. Do not let him take you dancing or talk you into any other activity that would require him to touch you. And don't be stupid and say to yourself, "I can handle this." Just don't let yourself get into a position where any handling is required. It is far too stressful plus, you somehow always come away feeling like dog-do.

If he has driven you to dinner, do not let him get out of his car at your hotel. Thank him for the ride and, if necessary, leap out of the car as it slows to a stop and dash into the hotel. If he walks you back to your hotel do not, under any circumstances, let him go any further than the elevator. If, God forbid, he leans forward to kiss you, step back, stick your hand out and shake his hand firmly while saying, "Goodbye", not "Goodnight".

4. The Platinum Rule (and this is a Rule, not a Tip) is never, ever, under any circumstance sleep with, or have sexual interaction of any nature whatsoever, with a client, married or otherwise. I do not care how good looking, how wealthy, how charming, or how anything he is. This is not an option.

If you are a professional, the reasons for this are apparent and need no further explanation. If you are not sure what they are, you don't have the sense to be let out of town by yourself. As my father was fond of saying, "You are softer than a sneaker full of whale shit."

Somedays, the Bear Gets You

"Things are going to get a lot worse
before they get worse."
-Lily Tomlin

One thing I have found is, as Abe Lincoln said, "You can fool some of the people some of the time," but, what I would add is, "You can never fool yourself for too long." If you find yourself thinking that that you have got it all under control – watch out. Never forget those sticks you are tossing up in the air on a daily basis are explosives and one little miss could have consequences of gargantuan proportion.

Fortunately, there are indicators that we receive or events that occur which serve as alarms and snap us out of our complacency. I am not talking about children getting arrested or husbands having affairs – those are leading indicators of really big problems. They are more like a personal Chernobyl. What I am talking about here are the reality checks that keep reminding us exactly what it is we are up against each day and that, despite what we continually tell ourselves, everything is always on the verge of spinning completely out of control. The trick is to keep it all on the verge and not let any spinning begin because, once it begins, there is no way to predict what will happen. The only thing certain is, it won't be pretty.

These indicators or warning events can be as simple as the previously mentioned throw-up down the back of your suit or the ever present runs in your panty hose as you are rushing into a meeting. Those horrible moments spent staring at the button on your blouse directly between your boobs, just waiting for them to make an appearance, as you realize that the little sound you heard was half of the button hitting the table in front of you, courtesy of your dry cleaner. You can't help but recall the fictional Murphy Brown announcing, "These babies haven't been out since Woodstock." and wondering if you would have the guts to say the same. There are also the times when you snapped open your briefcase in a very grown up, professional manner, ready to whip out the back up information that will prove your point beyond any dispute and wow the entire room and everyone in the room saw the coloring book and crayons your child had thoughtfully put in there for you. It does no good to explain that you have a three year old child. From that moment on, all of your colleagues believe that you color in your spare time which, although not a dishonorable thing to do, is not the image you have worked so long and hard to cultivate.

You can not stop your family life from colliding with your professional life. All you can do is attempt to minimize the damage. I recall the woman who wrote into *The Wall Street Journal* to share her story of the time she was picking up some clients at the train station. These were older, rather stodgy men without a great sense of humor.

She was congratulating herself on her foresight, thinking to ask her husband to trade cars for the day. His car was the nice, new Volvo, hers was the wreck filled with two year old gummy bears, french fries, and everything else that your children eat while in your car, leaving it smelling like the inside of a fast food restaurant. A car, where the interior could actually be of interest to the local board of health. No, she would not subject her clients to this and, because she was such a polished professional, simultaneously tossing all those sticks in the air, she had thought ahead, made allowances and brought her husband's car to the station to pick them up. Here we go, Wonder Woman, here we go.

As the train pulled up, she just happened to glance into the back seat to make sure there wasn't anything back there that would prevent her clients from sitting comfortably. Much to her horror, she realized that her daughters had left about fourteen, completely naked Barbie dolls all over the floor and seat. Only a parent could understand that it is possible to look at this scene fifteen times and only see it as your clients are coming down the steps of the train.

She was fairly certain that these gentlemen would not appreciate, or even begin to understand, how such a scene could be awaiting them. I was sitting in my office and laughing out loud reading her description of herself, scooping naked Barbies out of the backseat of the car, throwing them into the trunk, and trying to greet her clients as if nothing out of the ordinary had occurred. This is where we slip up. This scene – naked Barbies perched provocatively around her car was part of her life, something she saw everyday. But as far from her client's life as it possibly could have been. It would have been enough, in her opinion, to have changed their view of her professionalism. This is the sort of small thing that jolts us back to reality and forces us to admit that control is really not much more than an illusion or an unattainable Zen like state we can aspire to.

Another illustration of this, which I also nicked from *The Wall Street Journal*, illustrates that this crosses gender lines. In the old "misery loves company" spirit, I was actually pleased to learn this. It was one of the pieces that I clipped from the paper and had in a big pile that Captain Tidy threw away. I apologize for not having the date and by line but, I am fairly certain it was from Sue Shellenbarger's column. Although I have never even spoken to her, I feel as if I know her, I have been reading her column for so long. She is absolutely terrific, always on point and, in my opinion a true pioneer. She writes, among other things, the "Work and Family" column which currently appears on Wednesdays, in *The Wall Street Journal*. Anyway, I am pretty sure this was from one of her columns.

A man who worked for IBM was replying to a previous column that I had missed but, from what I could surmise from this particular column, it had been about people who work at home naked and get busted by, say, the Fed Ex guy or any unexpected visitor. I wanted to go back and find that column because it really sounded funny but, unfortunately, I never had the time to do so.

Anyway, this gentleman who worked for IBM wanted to make it very clear that when he worked at home, he was ALWAYS fully dressed. But, despite his attire, he could not prevent the inevitable collision with his real life.

It seems his office at home is in the basement, across from the laundry room. One morning he was in his office, changing the message on his voice mail, while his wife was across the hall folding laundry. His six year old daughter, unbeknownst to him, because he was working, had come down in search of panties.

When he played back his newly recorded message, making sure it was in keeping with the buttoned down world of IBM heard this:

In a clearly articulated very masculine voice, "Hello, you have reached He-Declined-to-Share-his-Name, at IBM. I am sorry, I can not come to the phone right now."

Then a very delighted feminine voice said, "Oh look, you don't have any clothes on. . . ."

He could change the message as many times as he wanted but he could never deny that the collision had occurred. If you believe that you can separate your family and your work, disaster is waiting right around the corner. It's the knowledge that we always have to bob and weave that keeps us on course.

That's not to say that we should stop trying. None of us can fully abandon the "Wonder Woman Complex" – it was too deeply ingrained. However, we are forced from time to time to admit that there are only twenty four hours in each day. That is incontrovertible. They are yours to do with whatever you'd like but, you only get twenty-four, no matter how smart or good looking you are. You really should try to use at least four, every day, for sleep.

There are so many things for which there is no preparation and not even my imaginary business school class could cover them all but, I sure as hell would get you a lot closer than any of the other classes they have out there.

One of the reasons for that is I do seem to be, for whatever inexplicable reason, one of those people to whom bizarre things happen, with an alarming frequency. I can't recount the times someone has said to me, "If anyone else told me that story, there is no way I would ever believe it. But you, I have no doubt it happened. In fact, you're probably leaving some of the really weird stuff out." I think it may have something to do with my karma or my rising moon, but I'm not certain.

Each time something really bizarre happens to me, it sets me back to the humble realization that I am always about fifteen seconds away from blowing my back porch off with a stick of dynamite. This is an unsettling feeling, nothing like an exhilarating adrenaline rush. It's much closer to pure terror.

I remember the time, not too long ago, that I was driving out of a major city, in a very large state in the Northeast, after hosting a business dinner, when my car just died. It was about eleven o'clock at night and I had the misfortune to have my car just stop working, without any warning, on a bridge that was under construction. The foreman on the job, a really sensitive guy, came marching over to my car and said, in an extremely irritated manner, "Hey, you can't leave your car here."

This is one of those times before you even open your mouth, you know the conversation is not going to be a positive one. As I was dialing AAA on my cell phone, I looked up at this nimrod and said, "WHAT? Do you actually think that this was my destination, that I drove up here and just turned my car off? My car died."

This was a guy who must have to get his information in written form because he just looked at me and nodding his head he said, "Lookit Honey, I just told you, you can't leave your car here."

My normally ladylike demeanor was taking a dive as I said, "Honey? Who are you, Fred Flintstone? Listen buddy, I just told you, MY F*&*%%*ING CAR JUST DIED."

Demonstrating that Darwin was definitely on to something,

this guy shouted at me, as he was walking away, "Sure, stay here. I am just telling you, you're going to get killed."

As I was sitting there, wondering if my company sponsored life insurance had a higher payout if I was killed on the job, a state police trooper drove up. As the officer strolled up to my car, I rolled down the window, and I could hear the foreman yelling at him, "I already told her, it's her fault if she gets killed."

As the trooper leaned into my window, I began to tell him my story. He asked how long ago I had called AAA and I told him that it had been about forty minutes since the call. At this point, the foreman came over and said to the trooper, "Hey, listen, I told this bitch that she had to move this car."

This was the only good thing that happened that evening. The officer turned to the foreman and said, "Who are you calling a bitch, asshole? Her car is dead – and it better be the only thing that dies on this bridge tonight. AM I CLEAR?"

Then he got on my car phone and "chatted" with the dispatcher at AAA, making it very clear that he expected someone here in the next five minutes. He told me that he couldn't stick around but, he would be back in a half hour and, if I was still there, he would take care of everything.

Relief flooded over me. That should always be a bad sign in a situation such as this but, I was so tired that I was, at least for a short time, lulled into complacency; a complacency that was shattered when I saw the two guys in the AAA truck. These guys could have been in *Deliverance*, had they been able to read. I had a sinking feeling that the foreman on the construction job had something to do with these two showing up.

I asked them to tow my car to a dealership, which the state trooper had given me directions to. I had no choice but to climb into the cab, between these two guys. When you climb into the cab of really big truck wearing a skirt, you have no choice other than to pull your skirt up high enough to lift your leg up to the first step. I do not have very long legs (another understatement). The two Deliverance men were actually making animal like sounds as I climbed over Deliverance I, to sit between them. Somehow, Deliverance II managed to reach between my legs, each time he had to shift gears. I was feeling as if I had sunk to an all new low but, little did I realize, the night was still young. Never let yourself think, "this is as bad as it gets" because, the gods will show you otherwise.

We got to the dealership and, as they were unloading my car from their flatbed, I was filling out one of those envelopes there for when you drop your car off after hours. I dropped my keys in and slipped it into the slot in the door of the service department.

I walked back to the truck, dreading the thought of getting back into the cab, between those two odious individuals. Not to worry. They informed me that it was "against the law" for them to take me anywhere other than the dealership. I informed them that on several occasions I had AAA tow truck drivers bring me home. They looked at one another, perhaps hoping for a thought to cross the empty terrain of their respective brains, and informed me that those guys had clearly been breaking the law. And then they drove away. It was now about 2 AM.

I had no choice other than to walk to a gas station. I have no idea how long that took but I can tell you that I felt like Dr. Zhivago, after he walked across Siberia, when I finally arrived at a Mobile station. It was the first time I had seen a drive-up pay phone. And, of course, there was not a phone book in sight.

Picture this: there I am, standing at a drive-up pay phone, begging an information operator to stay on the line with me, while I located a cab company that was open. Considering this was a major city, in a very large state in the Northeast, I was not prepared for every cab company to work bankers' hours. I finally got a live person to answer the phone, although it was clear that I had woken him up, he was alive. I explained my predicament and told him that I would give him $100 if he would come pick me up and stay with me until I found a hotel. He told me he was too drunk to come but, for $100 he would wake up his nephew and send him. I agreed without hesitation thinking, how much worse my night could possibly get?

I was about to find out. As I was talking to this guy on the phone, I see another guy staggering toward me. This guy was as drunk as you could possibly be and still be conscious. He also was missing most of his teeth and had the emaciated physique of a drug addict. He had not bathed in weeks and could have been anywhere between 30 and 75 years old. I could actually smell him before I could hear him. As he was approaching me, he was slurring out, "Hey Baby, how would you like to be my wife for the night?"

My limit had been passed hours earlier and I was probably temporarily insane; strictly in the legal sense so, the reality is, this guy is fortunate to still be alive. I looked at him and just flipped out. I won't even tell you what I said but, I can assure you, Maisey would not have been pleased to hear the language. I think that, even it his anesthetized state, I terrified him because, he slithered off like a frightened snake, but not before pointing out the flop house, where we could have a night of marital bliss.

I have never been gorgeous; beauty was never the first, second or third thing anyone would have ever mentioned about me, and I have always been well aware of this. Even bearing that in mind, I found myself standing there asking, "When did things ever get this slow, where an unspeakably vile, disgusting, stinking man such as this, would think he had a chance?" It was almost more than I could bear. Talk about an all time low.

When the taxi pulled up and it was a normal sixteen year old and his buddy, willing to help me out, I began to suspect a hallucination, similar to the dying man in the desert, imagining a steak dinner right in front of him. Or perhaps, the events of the evening had taken their cumulative toll and I had lost my mind altogether.

But, they were real and I am happy to report that, at nearly 3 AM, I was checking into a local hotel. They even gave me a little toothbrush and toothpaste. I could not have been more appreciative had it been the Hope diamond. The fact I had to get up at 5:30 AM could not dampen my overwhelming feelings of elation and success. I was so grateful to be in a clean bed, by myself, I didn't care what was going to happen in two and a half hours. Right then, I knew I was going to sleep. It is amazing how we can alter our expectations to fit the circumstances.

It is days like these when I am reminded of a client who raised ostriches. He raised them as a hobby but also because their feathers and eggs bring a great price in the market. The only wrinkle being the fact that it is extremely expensive to insure them because, they are so stupid they will run full force into a fence and break their necks, for no apparent reason.

As he was describing this to me, I grew somewhat alarmed as I heard my response of, "Perhaps they're not stupid, perhaps they've just had a really bad day."

I could see from the look on my client's face that he was considering the wisdom of his decision to let me manage his money. But, after we talked about it a bit, we both agreed that there were days when we could really relate to the ostriches' decision. Now that is another really scary thing they never discuss in business school. If I ever teach a course, I might call it, ""How to Avoid Acting Like an Ostrich, Even on Those Days You Feel Like One." I think it would be well attended, once the concept was understood.

I am sure that you have noticed from the title of this book, we are focusing on our children, careers, partners and our homes, as we carom through life, with the daily objective of not having anything blow up. The glaring omission is ourselves. While we are doing all of this juggling, who is paying attention to us? Forgive all of the rhetorical questions I have posed throughout this book. I do so because these are the questions that we don't allow ourselves to ask. Mainly because we don't have time or the answers are just too damn depressing.

The first thing that seems to go is sleep. In college it was only during exam periods that you suffered this deprivation and, you can soldier your way through nearly anything, if you know it is for a brief period of time. If you stayed up all night during Spring Break, you slept all day. It all evened out.

However, as we move forward in our lives, adding all of the essentials that we are certain we want, sleep is the first thing to be sacrificed. Then, one by one, each of those things you do, "just for you" begin to quietly fall away.

When you have a boyfriend, there is still plenty of time to exercise. Once he becomes a husband and you move to the suburbs, exercise (for you) becomes an event that must be planned, but it is still manageable, perhaps with less frequency. Then come the babies. Not even Wonder Woman can stay up all night with an infant, work all day at a job, come home to her family, cook dinner and go to the gym. What is the only part of that scenario that can be altered? Bingo – it's the gym. It's probably one of the most compelling reasons why Wonder Woman stayed single.

That's just the beginning. There was a time when I believed that I would always have a perfect manicure and pedicure. In fact, I couldn't believe that some women were so unconcerned with their appearance that they let these things go. (I know, I know – just shoot me; at least I am repentant and have publicly confessed.)

Well, being that these things take an entire Saturday morning or afternoon, need I say more? Even if the $100, without parking, isn't an issue, the time is. Time and sleep, sleep and time. It becomes a mantra of need.

But, we do continue to woodchuck along, don't we? Sometimes with better results than others. For example, last summer we had a black tie dinner dance to attend. It was a benefit for a local charity where I have served on the board and continue to support with great conviction.

At these types of event, I am always the woman who looks completely thrown together at the last minute. (There is a very good reason for that; it's because it's true.) I wanted this time to be different so, I tried to plan ahead. When I was in New York on business, I had about 20 or 30 minutes to spare and I flew into Neimans and bought a great dress. Luckily it fit, because I did not have time to try it on, a fact which horrified the saleswoman. She immediately identified me as a neophyte shopper and I think she was shocked when my credit card was accepted.

Making an extraordinary effort for this night to be absolutely wonderful, I also booked a facial for the afternoon of the event, with the idea of looking refreshed and generally much better than I usually do. As the woman was finishing up the facial, she asked if I was doing anything special that evening.

I told her happily that indeed I was. I would be at a fabulous black tie dinner dance, hosted by a couple who have an enormous home, directly on the ocean, with lots of my friends. The weather was set to be perfect and I was looking forward to having a ball. A regular Cinderella.

Her only response to my enthusiasm was to say, "Oh well then, I am sure you want me to wax your lip. . . ."

No, it had not been on my list of 1,507 things to do that day and I firmly told her not a chance; recounting the one and only experience I had with lip waxing, while still in college. It was a disaster and one I vowed I would never allow to be repeated.

She assured me that it was so long ago that I had been in college, things had changed a great deal. Of course, a thinking person would immediately challenge this by asking, "How much can hot wax change, in even 100 years?" and I did. She started telling me all this stuff about what they had added and taken away but, she really sealed the deal by making me feel as if I had a mustache that could have rivaled Groucho Marx's, which was definitely not the look I was going for.

Now I am going on record. NEVER AGAIN. I have very fair Irish skin that reacts violently to just about everything that touches it. I can now put hot wax on the top of that list. Not only did my entire lip swell – it looked as if I had collagen put over my lips rather than in them and, it was bright red. Maisey once had a lipstick color called "Cherries in the Snow" and that was the color of the swollen mass over my lip and under my nose.

I was nearly hysterical by the time I arrived home. I held ice on it, called my allergist who said to put cortisone cream on it, which I did but, nothing helped. Not even a little bit.

When I asked my husband just how badly it looked, hoping

for a little encouragement, he just shook his head and muttered something helpful like, "I'll never figure out why you women do shit like this." Apparently he was under the mistaken impression that it was a new fashion look I was going for.

You are probably wondering, "Why not just stay home?" It is a fair question and one I would ask myself, if anyone was recounting this pathetic tale to me. However, not only had we paid $500 for each of our tickets, we had invited guests as well so, there was no turning back. I knew that the wife of the couple we invited made her husband go out and buy a new tux, feeling his college model was not going to cut it. This was an obligatory event.

After a few glasses of wine, I tried to tell myself that perhaps it didn't look too badly and, working in my favor, it was beginning to get dark. That little self delusion was shattered when a woman that I don't know too well came over to talk with me. She was far too polite to ask me what the hell I had going on under my nose but, as we spoke, she kept running her thumb and index finger over her own upper lip. I don't even think she realized she was doing it.

There is a moral to this story, just as there is to most disasters. First and foremost, don't let anyone talk you into anything that your inner voice is advising against and, when you are juggling sticks of explosive, don't let one hit you in the face.

The Disconnects

"I don't think of them as chin hairs,
I think of them as stray eyebrows."
-Bette Midler

You can have an "ostrich kind of day" where everything just seems to go from bad to worse. I have found that it is best on such days not to step back and try to absorb the cumulative result of the disastrous events, as it can be overwhelming and lead to paralysis. It's best to take the advice Maisey's would give me, whenever I would be describing such an overwhelming chain of events to her.

In her beautiful brogue, she would say, "Ah Child, now calm down. Of course you'll be fine. Breathe a bit and we'll think about what the next step should be. It's just like eating an elephant – you take one bite at a time." It always made me feel better knowing that any situation, regardless of how large or how disastrous could be managed, by taking one bite at a time.

Perhaps it was the brogue or the authority with which she said everything but, I never thought to ask the obvious question, "Has there ever been a documented case of a person eating an elephant, ever?" That would of course be followed by a few more "If so, how long did it take?", "Why didn't the meat spoil?", "What exactly does elephant taste like?"

Like everyone else, I had seen plenty of fast African cats eating elephants on the *Wild Kingdom* but there seemed to be a defined pecking order, where everyone got a little, beginning with the cats and ending with the buzzards. Never once did I see a human involved in the eating.

To have made these observations to Maisey would have been pointless and served only to disappoint her, forcing her to accept that her granddaughter lacked imagination and the appreciation of metaphor. So, in her memory, and because it is now very clear to me precisely what it was she was talking about, I will tell you, "It's just like eating an elephant – take one bite at a time."

Despite all of the small bites and big plans there are times when you just miss. I refer to these as **The Disconnects**. These are different than an ostrich kind of day because that is a series of explosions in rapid order, where a disconnect is an isolated one. That's not to suggest it doesn't do damage. And, perhaps the greatest damage it does is to ourselves, as it leaves us wondering again, why we can't get it right all of the time. There are so many times when you do get it right but, it seems to be the blunders that so clearly stick out in your memory.

I will never forget when our oldest son was going to kindergarten. He would be leaving a pre-school he had been very comfortable at for three years and we wanted to make sure the transition was as smooth as possible. So, I did the 60's thing and read about 654 books on the topic and we spent the summer talking about how great kindergarten was going to be, what a big boy he was, and how exciting going to a new, big school was going to be. All very positive. All summer long.

We were high-fiving each other, congratulating ourselves on what great parents we were and how smooth the transition was going to be, all because we had made him so comfortable with the process. We were certain we had it all figured out.

We went shopping for the right lunch box – the metal *Return of the Jedi* number – picked out all of his new clothes together, because he was a "big boy" now and ordered the perfect backpack from L.L. Bean. There was nothing that we had not thought of and, the night before the first day of school, we went to bed with great confidence.

That confidence was shattered about 4 AM, when there was a little knock on our bedroom door and there was our "big boy", all dressed in his new clothes, clutching his lunch box and fighting back tears as he asked, "Well, when will I be seeing you again?"

As I am writing this, I have tears rolling down my face. Talk about a disconnect. I grabbed him, pulled him into our bed, lunch box and all, and as I hugged him, I felt like the worst mother in the world. Unfortunately for me, it would not be the last time.

The upshot is always the same. He had a great first day of school and I cried for three weeks each time I thought about it. He is almost 22 years old and I can still instantly recall his brave but sad little face, standing in our bedroom doorway. Although there have been others, many others, that is the one with him that will always hurt me the most, as I think about the poor little guy worrying all summer, as we were gaily prattling along, about kindergarten.

Do we learn from this? Of course, we swing totally in the other direction. When our youngest child entered kindergarten (recognizing a pattern here?) we barely mentioned anything about it. It was practically a state secret. Including the fact his big brother would be heading off to boarding school.

Although he had been along on the prep school swing

through New England with us, heard us arguing with his brother over getting the applications completed, went shopping for all the stuff for his dorm room, he never really made the connection that his big brother, his hero, would be living somewhere else.

Old oldest still says the most difficult part of being dropped off at boarding school was his five year old brother clinging to him and wailing, "You mean you aren't coming home with us?"

As soon as we got home, he took his 101 Dalmatians quilt off of his bed and into his brother's room, moved into his bed and slept there every night until his brother came home for Thanksgiving break.

It would seem that I have a great knack for either too much or too little information.

While we are on the topic of that same kindergarten/pre-school fall, one of the things that I delighted in was that our oldest son wanted to take the youngest shopping for his back to school stuff. What a treat for me, I would not have to battle a mall on a Saturday afternoon in August. Did I mention I am allergic to malls? Perhaps not allergic in the strict medical sense but; I hate lines, I hate crowds and having to suffer either has a direct negative effect on my otherwise cheery disposition. In fact, my children claim that I become almost unrecognizable to them. Perhaps not unlike my father in a sailboat race became to me.

In any event, I was overjoyed at the prospect of not having to do the back-to-school shopping, not to mention the opportunity it presented for brotherly bonding. I am sure that in my delirious joy I was deafened to Maisey whispering in my ear, "Child, whenever something seems too good to be true, chances are great that it is."

Her wise words came back to me as we were all escorting the baby into his new school for the first day of kindergarten. How proud I was, as I looked at my family thinking, "Well, we both may work but, here we are, on the first day of school, everyone is here, together, bringing him in." A regular Kodak moment. I am sure I was standing a little taller buoyed by self-congratulations.

I began to take notice of the other kindergarteners' backpacks. There was an approximate equal distribution of purple Barneys, pink Barbies, and multi-colored Power Rangers. And then there was my son with a black backpack with a carefully applied patch of the Grateful Dead skull, with the lightning bolt through it. It sort of stuck out.

I could take only a small measure of comfort in the fact that he is my youngest child and it would be my last "kindergarten disconnect". I knew then, I was getting far too old for this sort of thing.

But, of course, it doesn't end in kindergarten, unfortunately, it just accelerates as there are more and more things to remember each year they get older, and you are losing your mind at a similar rate. So, you find yourself needing to remember twice as much with half as much gray matter. How could this be considered fair?

There is Only So Much a Person My Age Can Remember

The only way you can survive a commute into Boston is to leave at the crack of dawn, otherwise you wouldn't get to work until noon, because of the traffic. Over the past 22 years I have had all sorts of arrangements to transport my children to school, far too many to even begin to list here, many cobbled together at the last minute. It was always best when we had a live-in nanny but, that was sporadic.

One morning I was sitting in my office about 7:45 AM and the phone rang. It was my youngest son's teacher, which was a bit alarming to me, as she had never called me at work. I anxiously asked her if everything was alright and she paused and said, "Well, not really. Not only is he not supposed to be here, we are closed today. You are supposed to be here for your parent-teacher conference."

There isn't a lot you can say when you find yourself in this sort of a circumstance so, in addition to feeling extremely foolish, I was thinking of how to fix the problem, not saying anything and she continued, "Well, you realize that he can't stay here. I am sure that the *other parents* will come to *their* conferences", making her opinion of me very clear.

"I'm thinking, I'm thinking," I said to her, as I was desperately trying to come up with someone I could call that could go get him and maybe keep him for the morning. Of course I had a meeting that I could not miss and my husband was out of town. That's the only time things like this ever happen.

Finally I sheepishly called my neighbor, one of the sweetest women in the entire world and she went and picked him up.

She has grown children, who do not have children of their own and our children don't have a grandmother so, she has adopted them. They call her Nanny and she is a gift from the gods. She assured me that she had no plans for the day and she "'would love to keep him." After work, as I guiltily went to her house to pick him up, they were making cookies and he announced he would not be going home with me, he was staying there. She has saved me so many times, I have no idea how I could have possibly gotten by without her. Each time she bailed me out, she would have me believe that there was nothing she would have rather been doing.

The Horror of Chin Hair or the Self-Disconnects

For me, chin hair was formerly thought to be the exclusive purview of the "Unclaimed Treasures" of my family. In some families, an elderly, never married aunt is referred to, somewhat derisively, as an "Old Maid". There is even a children's card game centered around this dreaded state of affairs, as the loser of the game is the one who ends up with the old maid. A game most certainly concocted by a man.

In many Irish families, to include mine, there were always several never-married aunts and great aunts, always ready to babysit and often in need of a ride to Mass. Rather than refer to them as "Old Maids" these ladies are called our "Unclaimed Treasures". Treasure or not, they were more than likely the source of the majority of our sightings of women with chin hairs.

Being that I never saw this unsightly condition on any married women, I concluded that it must have something to do with not being married and promptly forgot about it. That is, until one of my sisters-in-law, ever so tactfully mentioned to me how she had spotted a few on her chin and had to pluck them out. I was astonished. Here was this vision of loveliness; tall, thin, gorgeous and married; telling me that she had chin hair. I found myself speechless – something that doesn't often happen – and, as I was contemplating this new information, I may have nodded.

Then, I thought to myself, "Who has time to look at their chin? I am a mother, I have a job, I have. . . .oh no, do you suppose I have *CHIN HAIR?*"

I rushed into the bathroom, put my glasses on and stuck my face into the mirror. Much to my horror, there they were, practically a platoon of black hairs, growing out of my chin. I grabbed my tweezers and methodically eradicated the entire platoon, with a gusto equal to Sitting Bull descending upon the unsuspecting Custer, with the full knowledge that there were reinforcements ready to spring up to fill the fallen ranks. I have been scrutinizing my chin ever since. I am now up to a 5X magnification mirror with my glasses on and have extracted promises from my sons that when I can no longer see well enough to pluck unaided, they will do it for me.

After I had plucked to my satisfaction and calmed myself down, telling myself it didn't matter how many were there or how many people had seen them (oh sure), they were gone now. Then as I thought it over, I started laughing, wondering how my poor sister-in-law had drawn the short straw and ended up with the rotten job of telling me they were there. This is another instance of one of my sisters-in-law recognizing that I needed some sister love and she was there to give it to me. No matter how well you know and love someone, it is difficult to tell them they look like a fool. It takes a certain level of intimacy and I will be ever grateful that I share that with them. It is frightening to think what I would look like otherwise. I think they must get together and say, "What are we going to do about her?"

There are other seasonal disconnects which year after year repeated themselves, despite all of the preventative efforts I had undertaken the previous year. The one that jumps to mind is each winter, on the first really cold day of school, my children were always the only one without mittens or a hat because somehow they had evaporated over the summer. In late April, I would carefully put them away in the closet only to find no evidence of them the following November, when the temperature dropped to the teens for the first time.

Although I have no proof of this, I think they all leave together on a previously agreed upon summer night and go to the same place that the beach towels go to in the winter, each never to be heard from again. What other plausible explanation is there?

Degrees of Intimacy

As exciting as it must be to continue to have a series of new relationships, it takes a while to build up that level of intimacy or comfort where it's ok to show your warts or to see theirs. I am the first to say that it can work both ways when you let a man get too comfortable sometimes, there's no telling how he will behave. But, I can't imagine having dated someone three or four times and having them ask you to pull hair out of their ears or getting an attack of diarrhea. That is something I think I would definitely have to work up to. My husband, not recognizing this as intimacy, insists that I enjoy pulling the hair out of his ears because it hurts him. To hear him howl, you would think I was piercing his private parts.

One of my good buddies told me she knew it was time to end a long term affair when, one morning, they each reached over to the bedside table and put on the other's glasses. Actually it was the glasses and the huge bottle of laxative he began to bring along with him on their rendezvous. As she said to me, "Honey, the reason I have only slept with him all of these years and not married him is that there are some things I just don't want to know about." Amen to that.

In our effort to guard against the inevitable disconnects, one of our greatest weapons is having someone we can ask the intimate questions to, such as; "Do I have bad breath?", or to whom we can confide our greatest fears, without worrying about them running out the door screaming. It's having someone who will tell you the difficult things because they care about you, not because they want to see your feelings hurt. They truly want to protect you from those sort of blows delivered from the outside world. This is what I am talking about when I refer to "degrees of intimacy". The higher degree we can achieve, the better. This is nothing to take lightly and should be carefully considered when the decision to walk away is being contemplated.

Where Was I When. . . . ?

We need to accept, that even as early as our formative years, there were only so many hours in the day for us to learn and experience new stuff. I have no quarrel with all that I was fortunate enough to be exposed to and able to learn. Believe me when I tell you I know how lucky I was. However, you can never get it all and I seemed to have missed a great deal.

The school stuff always came fairly easily to me and I enjoyed it immensely; my family traveled a great deal which is always a wonderful learning experience; we also skied, sailed, participated in every imaginable water sport, rode horses and played lots of tennis and golf. I was taught to pour tea and the proper way to wear a hat and take my gloves off. So what's wrong with this, you are no doubt asking yourself. The answer is, nothing what-so-ever, but just like everything else, there is never enough time to get it all. What about all of the stuff I missed? The list goes on forever and, whenever I have an encounter with it, I am left feeling extremely unaccomplished. Why is it we seem to focus on what we can't do, rather than what we have done?

The first thing that comes to mind for me is make-up. Don't laugh, it's the truth. This is not something that is intuitive, it is definitely learned behavior. This may be genetic to the extent that it would appear that the skill is passed from one generation to another in the South but, I have come to believe that is an environmental factor rather than something written on your DNA.

My friend Linda, from Little Rock, can not believe that I have absolutely no make-up skill and sense. She believed that this skill was something that most women are born with or at least had some sort of knack for, until she met me, that is. She is still trying to digest my complete lack of natural ability in this area, as are my friends from New York City. They actually have suitcases that contain their make-up, with wheels on them. I can put all of my makeup in the pocket of my Levis and still have room for my license and a few dollars. My friend Sally says "Her face gets heavier every year." By "her face", I am sure that most of you realize, she is referring to her make-up and all the assorted creams and accoutrements she employs to keep herself so beautiful. It works, cause she is beautiful and I wish I knew how to do the same for myself. It's just that I never think I look like me when I have anything more than a little lipstick and perhaps mascara on.

This is most certainly a disconnect of mine, because I don't have a clue on how any of those powders, creams, liquids and brushes work together, despite the great patience of the fabulous Fran, my person at the Chanel counter at the local mall. Fran has spent numerous hours attempting to instruct me in the proper application of each of these substances and the proper tools required for each. I have spent a small fortune on all of the tools and powders, liquids and solids that you apply with the tools. She even scheduled me for an appointment with the "expert from headquarters" who came in to do "make-up consultations" with only their best clients. I think I was a major disappointment.

After she carefully explained and applied each different concoction, telling me emphatically how important it was to only use the proper brush or tool with each, she was finally done and, more than likely, exhausted. She triumphantly turned the mirror to me and said, "How do you think you look?"

I couldn't help it, I had to be honest and I blurt out, "Like a hooker." I think perhaps I am one of those women for whom make-up is just not the right way to go. That's not to say that there are not many flaws which deserve covering, which is most surely the truth. I have lots of those little veins on my cheeks and they are always the first thing that Fran, and other courageous make-up women who preceded her, tried to help me cover. I try to tell them that, with my pale Irish skin, it's the first time in my life I have had color in my cheeks. They are appalled that I am ok with the idea of everyone seeing all these little veins and regarding them as some sort of natural coloring.

I do realize that, if properly applied, make-up would make me look much better. It's just that I don't like the way all of my flaws look covered. It looks too fake. Plus, what happens when someone who is accustomed to seeing you all made-up, sees you without any of it on? Are they shocked? Are they ever frightened? Are any of them on record, running out of the room screaming?

At the health club where I work out, I am absolutely astonished to see these cute youngins putting make-up on before they work out. I don't know about them but I get so sweaty when I work out I would be afraid that halfway though my workout it would congeal into some sort of unnatural mass, that I would find impossible to remove. Or, alternatively, it could mix with the sweat and start dripping off my face, resembling those mud slides they had in Southern California where entire houses slid into the bay.

I don't care what you think about Hilary Clinton personally or politically; she would understand what I am talking about and I very much appreciated it when she said something like, "I don't know what I was doing at all of those sleepovers when everyone was putting on make-up and fixing their hair, but I sure wasn't participating." I don't know what I was doing either but, it sure as hell was not learning about make-up and hair-dos. It's embarrassing. Well, actually, it's just another disconnect.

I realize that the perpetual state of disorder in evidence throughout my house is a disconnect but, there are some things that, even in light of the constant state of chaos my house is in, still stick out as being a real miss. One would be the "dog print".

Our town has a very big Fourth of July parade which happens to pass by the end of our street. For many years we hosted a brunch and parade watching extravaganza. These always went much smoother when the holiday was on a Sunday or Monday, giving me a day and a night to prepare. In spite of the day it fell on, I'd seem to pull it off, year after year; some years more successfully than others.

I remember one year, after the parade, there were a bunch of folks who came back to our house for another round of food and drinks and they were sitting in our living room chatting. I walked into the room to see if anyone wanted anything and I observed one of our guests, who keeps her house sparkling clean, staring at the rug in our living room in absolute horror.

At the time we had Casey, our beloved golden retriever. I don't know how much you know about dogs but, these guys have really long blond hair and they spend most of the summer shedding globs of it. As I looked to see what could possible be the reason for her distress, I saw the body print of Casey. You know how the police draw a line around a dead body on the sidewalk? Well Casey had left a similar print of himself, in dog hair, on the living room rug. Actually there was dog hair on everything but this was where it was actually in a defined shape – that of a running dog. It could have been considered a work of art by some, obviously my guest was not one of those people. Oh well, I guess I forgot to vacuum before everyone arrived.

What Would Joan Do?

Although I am able to reluctantly accept that my life will always be fraught with disconnects, that does not mean that I am not constantly on the look out for ways to diminish the likelihood of having one occur. The best way to do this is by watching and learning from everyone around you, all of your life. The more open you are to learning from others, surprise, the more you will learn. Take every opportunity presented to you to observe. Sometimes learning what not to do, can be more valuable that learning the proper way to do something.

Let's face it; we completely dismiss anything said to us by our parents, by way of instruction or advice, until we are adults. The same pretty much goes for teachers, although if you are fortunate enough to have had one or two that you regarded so highly, you actually listened to and took some of their advice, well, good for you. You are ahead of many of us. We always listened to our friends, with mixed results, often because they tell us what we want to hear.

So who else is there? I would suggest that you will never have a boss from whom something can't be learned, even if it's the "don'ts of management".

I have been pretty fortunate in this department; throughout my career I have had a fairly good series of bosses, with a few clunkers thrown in. At this stage in my career, I have the luxury of being able to refuse to work for anyone whom I don't respect both professionally and as well as personally. I do realize how fortunate I am for this and please understand, it wasn't always the case.

The boss I have now is a media star. His name is Hugh Johnson (not the wine guy) and if you ever watch *CNBC, CNN, Money Line* or any assortment of shows on television that feature the capital markets, you would recognize him. He is the handsome, somewhat avuncular guy who has the ability to make you feel that he is sitting at your kitchen table talking with you, rather than on national television. I have learned more from him about the capital markets that any other ten people I know, combined. He is a great guy and I love working for him. He has a really good sense of humor and he works really hard, always keeping our clients' needs foremost in any decision we make. A day doesn't go by when I don't learn something from him. I would never tell him this though, it would just swell his head and he would become unbearable. I have no fear of him reading this book because he only reads things of a financial nature. So, if you know him, don't blow my cover, please.

Previous to Hugh, I had perhaps the toughest boss I have ever had in my career. She was a perfectionist and she demanded perfection from everyone who worked for her and would let you know, in very clear, undampened terms, if she felt you had not made the grade. This lent itself to some rather tense meetings but, I kind of liked it because she forced us all to continually raise the bar. No one ever came to a meeting unprepared, unless they had a death wish. Also, she worked along side you, just as hard, setting a standard for all of us.

Although I would refer to her as "the Grand Fromage" to my people (a name that I shared with her, much to her delight) her name is Joan. She is married to the wonderful Philip, who would entertain us all at firm parties, by telling us stories of her reaming out some unsuspecting person. She would listen to the story, amused that he was telling it to us and then say something like, "Well, what did they expect? They did it wrong or they were late or too fast or too slow. . . ."

I learned so much from her about many things but two in particular; confidence and details. I am not good at self promotion, never will be, it just runs against my whole being. However, she beat into me how important it is to go into every meeting, regardless of the purpose, with the idea that you are just going to blow everyone in the room away, by how good you are.

We were acquired by a much larger company when we worked together and, during the entire acquisition period there were many meetings and presentations. I remember one time she grabbed me by the shoulders before we went into a particularly important one, put her face about three inches away from mine, looked me in the eye and fiercely said, "Mimi, it is up to you and only you, to make each one of the men in that room realize you are the very best chief investment officer they will ever see. I don't give a crap about how you were raised and what was said to you growing up. It's time to be tough."

It was the best presentation that I had ever made, up to that point in my career, and I have never forgotten her words. When I am faced with a presentation or meeting that for whatever reason has me stressed, I can conjure her up, holding my shoulders and looking me in the eye and it always gives me strength. What I am trying to say is, some people allow themselves to be terrified by a boss like Joan and, they are always running for cover. That is such a waste. I am telling you, step up and learn from them, if you are ever fortunate to find yourself working for one.

I consider myself somewhat Type A and a perfectionist to whom details have always mattered, but compared to Joan, I am a slob. She is one of those people who is able to think of every eventuality and plan for it and never can understand someone who doesn't. I can not tell you how many times, by asking myself, "What would Joan do?" I have been able to figure out the best way to approach a complex problem or handle a tough situation. It is a standard which I will never relax, despite the fact it tends to drive everyone around me crazy.

I am sure that it will come as no surprise to you to learn that she has risen to a very high level in the company that acquired our small firm and I suspect it won't long before she is running the world, or at least North America. When that happens, I am sure it will be a much better organized place.

Guidlines and Remedies

"Laugh and the world laughs with you.
Cry and you cry with your girlfriends."
-Laurie Kuslansky

As I stated in the Introduction, the state of "permanent balance" does not exist in this universe for anyone with a child, partner, house and a job. Do not delude yourself. To try to achieve such will only serve to hasten the final break-down of your mental faculties. Picture a dog chasing his tail.

Accepting that permanent balance is not an option, we have to grab whatever moments of temporary balance we can. For each of us, there is something that can bring us into a blissful state of peace, leaving us feeling, at least for that moment, that all of our stars and moons are aligned. I felt that way when I held each of my children for the first time. But, as we know, you can only hold a baby for the first time once. Becoming Old Mother Hubbard would have left me permanently unbalanced, despite those many moments of bliss so, I had to find another source of temporary balance.

The good news is, the source I have discovered to bring me into a state of balance, albeit temporary, is plentiful and the only cost associated with it is time. Yeah, yeah, yeah, I know, "time is money" but at least it doesn't have to come out of your wallet. I'll bet the sharpest of you have already guessed. It is having female friends. There is nothing like it. Most straight men do not understand the concept of friendship with a woman because, in the back of their mind, they are always wondering what the odds are that the woman might agree to sleep with them.

This distraction of theirs really gets in the way of developing anything of a deep nature. I have finally gotten incontrovertible evidence that it is not their fault – as it were, I am moving from theory to law. The proof was of the most personal nature to me and one that truly knocked me clear off my feet. I believe that I have not fully digested it.

My family, minus the oldest son, went on a vacation out West to a dude ranch. One of the wranglers (those are the people that take care of the horses and such), by the lovely name of Coventry, was an absolutely delightful young lady who also happened to be train wreck good looking. My husband, who can at times suffer from a completely over developed sense of optimism, insisted on having his picture taken with her, several times. When we got home I was showing the pictures to my son and told him the great news. Coventry was going to a college very close to where we live and that she would love to meet him. He looked at me, shaking his head, reminding me he had a girlfriend. I said that I was well aware of that and this young lady had a boyfriend but, she would be a great friend for him to have. He left me wondering how I could have possibly failed him so miserably, when he looked at me and stated quite emphatically and without apology, "Mum, it is impossible to be friends with a girl that looks like that cause the entire time you are with her, you are trying to get her into bed." My very own son said this. If someone could come out of my household, not to mention my womb, thinking this, it has to be hard wired. The fact that this boy has been listening to me for 20+ years and yet he remains on that one dimensional plane, confirmed to me what I have always suspected. There is no hope. It's another one of those DNA things, like the fact that ducks are born knowing how to swim. I had to go lie down.

That's why we have to stick together, we women. I don't care if we call ourselves women, ladies, girls, babes, chicks, whatever. That seems to be more of a regional preference. I know my good friends from the South are always girls, as are the women I met in Ireland. We Yankees tend to think of ourselves as women. Unfortunately, ever since Jean Harris' book was published, whenever I hear the term ladies, I think of prisoners. Maisey would not be pleased to hear this. She felt that to be a lady was the bare minimum of acceptable female behavior, which included but was not limited to, conducting oneself in a ladylike manner in all circumstances. This was, to her way of thinking, one of the corner stones of a life well lived and nothing at all to be taken lightly.

Regardless of what we call ourselves, it is our friends that provide the glue that often holds our lives together. They are the ones who call you when one of your children gets suspended from school for drinking or wrecks one of your cars, to tell you they just found the sweetest picture of that very child at the age of three on Halloween, dressed as a dinosaur. They also make a point to tell you that your ex-husband's new wife's rear end is expanding at light speed and that she is so stupid she could be the single source of all blonde jokes. They always have wine and frequently have tequila.

You can laugh and cry with them at the same time, believe that they will keep your secrets and know that they will love you no matter how much weight you have gained. I am not talking about faux-friends here; those people that try to cozy up to you to learn something about someone else, or want to be your friend because they think you know the right people and go to the right parties. Faux-friends can be flushed (and that is the right word) out quite easily. They are in the relationship for only one reason, to advance themselves. That is a difficult thing to hide. They are the ones who tell you they just don't know which bikini to wear, directly after you have confided in them that you can not, whatever drastic measures you employ, loose those 30 pounds that have mysteriously gathered around the area between your knees and your bellybutton. They ask you hurtful questions they already know the answers to and feign, first shock, then sympathy, at your response. When they are sitting in your living room, listening to you pour your broken heart out, they are not even trying to make you feel better because all they can think about is who they are going to call as soon as they leave, to report every last word you have told them. They phone you when they hear you have a terminal illness or that your husband is having an affair, even though they have never called you before. They can take no pleasure in your children's successes and they covet everything you have, including, in most cases, your husband. Fortunately they show themselves early in the game, before they have had the opportunity to inflict too much damage. They tend to travel in bunches so, beware. If you do get tangled up with one of these, don't feel too badly. It has happened to all of us and it just makes our real friends all the more precious.

Friendship is not all fun and games. There is a certain responsibility incumbent with the mantle of being a true friend. We must, whenever possible, protect our friends from any type of pain or harm. This is not always easy. I have found that when we are most in need of protection there is an equal and opposite force in the universe that renders us the least receptive to friendly intervention. But, as a true friend, you must be strong. You never know when you will be in need of some tactical intervention in one of your plans and it is only a true friend who will butt in at the crucial time and gently point to the flaws in your thinking.

To this end, there are some guidelines that we must be certain that we and all of our friends understand and, whenever possible, follow. In some places, these would be called rules. However, I have never liked rules and my first tendency when introduced to one is to break it. So, these are not rules but rather guidelines. Albeit, guidelines that, whenever possible, should be followed. There are times, if you are really a good true friend, you may be called upon to enforce one or more of these guidelines. Familiarity with them before the sticky situation arises can be very helpful. For instance, rather than being forced to explain the whole "guideline-thing" in a situation where you may be pressed for time, it is much more effective to say, "No, you can't possible do that......it's Guideline #4." Presumably, your friend has not only acquainted herself with the guidelines but she has taken the next step and bought into the guidelines, at least at the time she was reading them. Sometimes that is all that you need. Your friend will immediately reach a state of clarity and say, "Oh ma gawd, #4. . .what was I thinking? Oh ma gawd, thank you." Sometimes it is a bit more difficult and you have to use other tactics of persuasion, such as reminding your friend the result of another friend who broke the same guideline and has never been quite the same. Lastly, and it really is the final measure, there is physical restraint. Often, this measure requires the assistance of another similarly committed friend and should be employed only when all else fails.

These guidelines fall under some general categories. Commitment to these guidelines has saved thousands of women untold hours of pain and public humiliation. Study them, learn them, follow them and share them with those you love. I would be most appreciative to hear from those of you who have any of your own, which have proved to be essential. These are things that true friends share.

All of the following guidelines assume that our friends are not being abused either physically or emotional but rather suffering a temporary lapse in their otherwise stellar judgment. If one of your friends is being abused in any manner, you must take every possible measure to make her safe. There are no exceptions.

COMMUNICATION:

1. Never mail a letter that was written fewer than 24 hours after drinking tequila. Make that any alcohol at all.

2. Never call your boss at home. Never. No matter how bad your day was or how stupid he/she is. It is career limiting.

3. Never call an old boyfriend "by mistake", expressing shock and disbelief that you dialed his number, all the time secretly hoping that the sound of your voice will kindle that old flame. It will only make you appear more pathetic in his eyes. Better to listen to Bonnie Raitt singing, "Love Has No Pride" and drink a pitcher of margaritas with friends.

4. Never ever confess to an affair. No matter how understanding your man pretends to be at the time, he will never forgive nor will he forget. He will also consider it a license to have his own affair, which is something you do not, under any circumstances, want to provide to him. I have no idea who made up that ridiculous, "honesty is always the best policy" thing but, if I ever meet him, I'll kick his ass.

5. When your new boyfriend asks you if he is better in bed than your old boyfriend, regardless of the truth, do not pause, do not ponder; just say with great enthusiasm, "Oh yes, much better." Should you find yourself in that unfortunate position where this is not the truth, perhaps you need to rethink things.

6. Never ever tell a friend that she has gained weight, no matter how many times she asks you. She has a scale, believe me, she knows. She just needs to hear that she still looks good to you. Self esteem gets us 90% of the way there, regardless of where that might be and it is our duty, to fill our friends right up to the ears with good feelings. Lord knows, the rest of the world is quick enough to tear them down.

7. Never give parenting advice to anyone to whom you haven't been married.

8. Never take any sport lessons from someone you are sleeping with.

9. No matter how angry you are, never follow a man out to the driveway to continue an argument. It's trashy. Use the time away from him productively. Use it to tighten up your arguments.

10. No matter how angry you are, only say what you truly mean and want him to know. It's much easier to remember and, if you said something truly terrible, and it was true, you might just be giving yourself a wake up call.

MEN

11. When our friends are in love, no matter what we truly feel, their men are great and, this is important, off limits. When their men are rotten to them, they are bums. And still off limits.

12. Do not try to reason with a man, they do not have the software. Logic is not consistent with a group of people that would consider tractor pulling to be an athletic event.

13. When you know, for absolutely certain, beyond a shadow of a doubt, that a man is stepping out on one of your very close friends, you have to tell her. God knows everyone else in town is dying to; it should come from someone who loves her. Just be absolutely certain because this is one of those few times from which you can never recover, if you are mistaken.

14. Never trash a friend's man, no matter what she is saying about him. Listen to her. Support her. Love her. But don't tell her what you really think of him because when they are kissing again she will remember all the rotten things you said about him, forgetting entirely all the stuff she said and be mad at you. If they actually get divorced, once it is final, you can say everything you have been holding in the entire time they were together, but only if you are absolutely certain that the divorce isn't just a temporary thing.

15. Never let a man take your picture naked. He will plead with you, tell you they are "just for him, he won't show them to anyone". He will lie. They can't help it; they have to show their friends and anyone else in the locker room or bar, or

wherever he was when they just "fell out". I haven't quite figured out why but it does seem to be a universal truth. The only exception to this guideline is when the man is a plastic surgeon that you have hired, not one you are dating.

16. Don't try to understand the locker-room-thing. It's one of those things you just have to accept, much like the speed of light. In a locker room, a man is transformed into an entirely different life form. Once a man enters a locker room, he can remember the score of any athletic event ever played anywhere in the world. He can remember who scored each point and who made the errors. He also can remember the name of each player who has ever played a professional, college or local high school sport. My friend, Lucy, says it is like living with men with "Reverse Alzheimer's" disease.

A locker room is the only place where it is acceptable to be touched by another man, in any stage of undress. They enjoy standing around chatting naked. It must make them feel manly. I refer to it as "fanny time". Please be assured, there is nothing, God forbid, sexual in any of this behavior. The only sexual overtones are those when they freely share all of the intimate details of your relationship, especially if you have a skill or talent they feel may be of particular interest to their friends, placing them in a position of great envy. Please understand, this may or may not reflect the reality of what actually occurs within your relationship, just what will pass for truth in the locker room.

Passing gas is judged in a manner similar to an Olympic competition and, just like all three year olds, they share with great pride, that they went poopy. It is a current day example of "Culture in Decline", not unlike the Roman

Empire, close to it's demise.

17. Never have sex with your boss or his boss. If this guideline requires any further explanation, you are probably very young and in desperate need of the wise council of older women. Generally speaking, sex at work is a bad idea. You think no one knows and the truth is, everyone knows. Then when it's over, making a bad situation worse, you have to see him every day. One of my friends was the head of facilities at a very large company which had cameras in their stairways, as part of their security system. Well, sure enough, one day she gets a call from the security guys who are just killing themselves laughing. She goes down to their offices to find out what is so funny and finds them watching a tape, taken right in the company stairwell. As you might have guessed, it is a man and a woman, doing the deed, right there in full view of the camera. But, what struck my friend as the most preposterous thing of all was, there was this young woman, bolicky-bare-ass as the day she was born and the guy, get this, had not even loosened his tie! Now that's a girl that needs a true friend.

18. It is never a good idea to sleep with one of his friends, just to show him what's up because, strangely, the guys will forgive each other and both think you're a slut.

19. Don't drive by his house, after it's over, with the hope of a "sighting" or even worse, trying to see whose car is in his driveway. If he sees you it will be utterly humiliating for you and merely affirm his decision. The quintessential lose/lose for you.

20. Talk long and hard with your friends, then a really good

lawyer, before you sign any sort of a pre-nuptial agreement. How can you possibly be compensated for your youth? I don't care how much money he has. Just make sure you get a big chunk because you will never be 30 again.

21. If you are in the market for a new man, regardless of how injured you are, be choosey. Don't just settle for the first warm body with a pulse. As I told a very dear friend of mine, coming off a second divorce, when asked what I thought about the new play thing, I could only say, "When you are in the airport, waiting for your bags, you don't take the first one that rolls by, you wait for the one with your name on it. There are many reasons for this the most obvious being that everything in that bag fits you and they are all the colors that you are the most comfortable with." There are times when you are forced to resort to metaphor, rather than hurt a friend. However, I do hope you understand what I am trying to tell you here.

In fact, I am not entirely sure my friend understood what I was saying but, being that he is a man, that is not so difficult to understand. This is an extremely intelligent guy, in fact one of the brightest I have ever known, at least as far as books go. But with relationships, he is still learning. For instance, when he was married to his second wife, he bought a house for them to live in. When they got divorced, he lost the house. Then, his former wife wanted to sell the house so, guess what he did? He bought it AGAIN and moved into it with his new girlfriend, whom I happen to be very fond of. But, regardless of how I feel about her it doesn't change the fact that he is lining up to be the first guy I have ever known to lose the exact same house twice. There is a comedian out there, who says in one of his routines, "I am never getting married again, I am just going to find a woman I don't like and buy her a house." And buy it and buy it. . . .

PARENTING

22. When your children are babies do not, under any circumstances, ever utter the words (always spoken dripping with contempt), "My child would NEVER. . ." because I can promise you, that sweet little baby will not be a baby forever. They will grow into a child that will make you eat every single word.

I remember the time, when our oldest child was in the 8th grade, my husband and I were having lunch with dear friends, a generation older than we. They were saying what a nice boy he was and I smiled proudly and nodded my head saying confidently, "And he has not given us one minute of trouble." The two of them looked at each other with, "Can she possibly be this naïve?" written all over their faces. Finally the wife looked at me, and said with great conviction, "Oh dear, it just hasn't started." Because they are good friends, they have never once reminded me of this.

23. Don't expect your children to either relive your athletic glory or, even worse, make up for your lack of athletic glory. It is pitiful and embarrassing to your child.

24. Never speak to one of your children's volunteer coaches unless to say either "thank you" or "Is there anything I can do to help?" Review rule directly above.

25. When they are teenagers don't try to sell them. You would never recover your investment. Plus, it's illegal in most states.

26. As tough as it can be, remember at all times, who is the parent and who is the child. It still baffles me, when I go in to break up a ridiculous argument my husband is having with one of the children and he says to me, "Well, he started it." I wish I had a dollar for every time I have asked that man, "How old are you and how old is he?"

27. Never mention that you do not like one of your children's friends. That knowledge makes them irresistible to your child. Triple that if we are talking about a dating relationship.

28. Halloween is not a competition among mothers. It is a night for your children to binge on candy given to them by strangers. Enough said.

29. I have seen, in one of those pieces that seems to float through the Internet, a wonderful bit of parenting advice and I will share it with you. "Never raise a hand to one your children. It leaves your genitals unprotected." Something to think about anyway.

30. Do not knock yourself out over your child's pre-school admission process. The preschool they go to will not have any impact what so ever on the quality of their adult life, including what institute of higher learning they attend.

I have a friend, who lives in Manhattan (you may be thinking, "well that explains a lot", but don't be so quick to judge) who grilled her sweet little three year old on any possible topic he could have been asked at his interview. He probably could go on "Who Wants to be a Millionaire". I am surprised she didn't take a leave of absence from work. After the interview she was debriefing (her word) him, forcing him to repeat, verbatim, the interview. When he told her the admissions director asked him what his favorite vegetable was, she was particularly pleased. Recognizing that her son had never let a vegetable onto his highly selective pallet, she had anticipated this question and prepped him. So, when she asked him what he responded, she was not at all surprised to hear, "poi puree". Absolutely beaming, she asked him, "What did Mrs. Admissions-Person say?" more than likely anticipating that it was an instantaneous acceptance to the school. He looked at her with his sweet little face and said rather matter-of-factly, as only a three year old can, "She asked me what poi puree was and, I told her I had no idea." I'm not sure my friend as ever been quite the same but, the good news is, although he was not accepted at this pre-school, he is a terrifically well adjusted fourteen year old, attending a wonderful school in Manhattan. He has still never eaten a pea, pureed or otherwise.

31. Read to them. It is one of those rare gifts where the giver receives more than the getter. They snuggle up next to you; you can smell the fresh shampoo on their heads whenever you want and they don't think you are being weird and, best of all, you teach them to love reading. The books they have for children now are illustrated for the children and written for the parents. It is something they will always remember, but not nearly as vividly as you. Those memories really help when they are teenagers.

32. When you are teaching them how to drive, just have faith that someday you will be 94 years old and driving them somewhere, stubbornly insisting that you can, without a doubt, drive as well as they did when they were 17, perhaps even a bit better. If you really want to get them, drive one of

their cars and see how they like it. I know it probably seems like a long time to wait for the payoff but, trust me, the way the years have been spinning by, I am certain I will be 94 in no time at all.

Even with the gift of great friends and a strict adherence to "The Guidelines", injuries occur. Unfortunately, they are unavoidable from time to time. Although at the moment it is happening you may feel that your very life is in danger; that you could just keel over from the pain and suffering that has befallen you, I assure you, with friends and time, you will recover. Although time truly does dampen all of our pain, for some of us, tequila has been known to speed the process along.

What follows is a list – again I do not claim it to be exhaustive, and would love to hear from you about those remedies that I have over looked – detailing remedies or cures, some which can be undertaken alone and some allow for group healing. They work, and the sun will shine for you again. In the meantime, these are some steps you can take to expedite your return to harmony.

REMEDIES:

1. There is almost no problem in the world that can not be helped by chocolate or tequila. Keep plenty of both on hand at all times and dispense freely. In a pinch, wine can serve as a substitute but don't try putting it into your blender.

2. Allow someone to really fuss over you. Whatever your pleasure is, either to go out and get a massage by some 22 year old hunka-hunka burning love or get one of those great

facials with all kinds of fruits and healing herbs, or a manicure and pedicure. Find one of those new wild colors and you'll feel like a new woman. Plus, when you are hurting inside, someone working really hard on the outside can make you feel a whole lot better.

Or splurge on a new hair style or hair color, making you feel all new and gorgeous. Be careful here; better bring a friend along for the objective opinion. You live with a hairdo a lot longer than toe-nail polish and we are working on things that will make you feel better, not reaffirm every lousy decision you have ever made.

3. Road trips are good for the aching soul. There is nothing like a change of zip code to use as an excuse for misbehaving. Often misbehaving is the first step to healing or, if done to a sufficient degree can be directly attributed to forgetting entirely the debacle from which you have just extricated yourself.

4. If your job or your children make a road trip impossible, a long hot bubble bath, with a vat of wine, goes a long way.

5. Making a voodoo doll can be very therapeutic. Get your friends to help, it becomes a much more creative process. I assure you, they will think of things that would have never even crossed your mind. They are just dying for the creative outlet to express these inspirations. Involve large quantities of alcohol.

6. Expensive champagne makes you feel like a princess and, it is appropriately served at any time of day, to include breakfast. Best to mix with orange juice if you want to make

it to lunch.

7. This is one of my favorites. Get your girlfriends together and go out dancing. Put your red dress on, shine up your cowboy boots and go find a great band playing in a honky-tonk bar. Dance all night but leave only with those with whom you arrived. We are talking Remedies here, not the start of new problems.

8. No matter what – get out of bed, brush your teeth, take a shower and wash your hair. After that, you can go back to bed if you really want to but, I can nearly guarantee that you won't want to because you'll know you're in charge. And that is really what healing is about, knowing you are in charge. Someone has done you wrong, sure enough. But, it's only a temporary setback. Once you realize that you are back in control, your healing has begun.

I have to admit, if you are horribly hung over, you may not feel entirely in charge. What I recommend is greasy food – fried eggs with lots of mayo and great big slice of Bermuda onion always sets me on my way but, it is strictly a matter of preference. (Hopefully, this is not your first major hangover and you have some sort of idea what works for you.) My good friend Linda, who is from Little Rock, just pops open a can or two of Coca-Cola – don't know how she does it but she swears by it. She calls it, "the Breakfast of Champions". Perhaps someday they will consider putting her picture on the front of a Coke can. Wouldn't that be something? Makes me smile just thinking about it.

9. Now this next suggestion could be either a remedy or the beginning of another problem and that really depends on

you. It is clearly not for everyone. I have several friends for whom it has worked quite nicely but, they were willing to put up with the disapproving stares or, as an alternative, operate only in the dark. They claim the great sex makes up for all of the negative surface noise.

If you are the least bit unsure, my advice, for whatever it is worth, would be not to go with this particular remedy. However, if you are like one of my friends who just didn't care at all what anyone thought, who was just along for the joyful ride, well then, if the situation presents itself, I say, "go for it."

I know you are asking yourself, "What the hell is she rambling on about? The answer is, finding yourself a "Boy Toy", or a "Little Love Child". Make sure he is at least 21 years of age so you don't get arrested for buying him beer. That would not only be extremely embarrassing, it would be awfully difficult to explain to the compliance people at work, if you are employed as I am, in the securities business and forced to report any personal infraction of the law.

One of my buddies, who is a professional photographer, a business not regulated by any government bureaucracy, did just that one spring time when she found herself very bored and in need of some really good lovin'. The age difference did not bother her at all she claimed, although she did try an extraordinary justification of their "visual age difference" being much less than the actual 20 years it was because she looked much younger and he looked much older than their respective years. I listened carefully as she explained this to me and applauded her creative rationalization.

I think this, combined with the fact she really didn't care, was working quite nicely, until she decided to buy a new car. She and the Boy Toy went to a Saab dealership and after looking around for a while, she found the car she wanted to test drive.

The salesman walked up to them and agreed that she could take the car for a test drive. My friend and her Love Child were each getting into the front when the salesman said to Love Child, "Why don't you hop in the back and I'll ride up front with Mom."

She is now driving a new Volvo.

10. This next remedy takes a little bit of time, which is why I put it near the end of the list. Trust me though, it is all about you being in charge that really makes you feel good about yourself. Now if you are one of those perfectly-in-shape-youngins go out and get a hot fudge sundae and skip this remedy. It will not apply to you. However, for the rest of us, there is nothing like losing five pounds to make you realize that you are in control of your life. Slipping on a skirt or into a pair of jeans that previously required a crow bar and three friends to make it happen, really lets you know that, at the end of it all, no one but you is pulling the strings. You can do whatever it takes. Now that is a good feeling indeed.

11. And finally a remedy taught to me by my previously mentioned girlfriend from Little Rock, Linda. She gave me a tiara for one of my birthdays – our birthdays happen to be one day apart so, she brought hers along for the celebration. My husband was aghast that we were actually going to wear them into a fancy restaurant in Boston but, he is also slightly afraid of all southern women, so he just rolled his

eyes and drank plenty of single malt scotch.

Linda told me that she always brings a tiara to a birthday party and, the birthday girl is always delighted. She then told me, she just leaves her tiara next to the telephone and, if she is having a bad day and feeling blue, she just puts the tiara on and, what do you know – she feels like a princess. It's worth a try, I mean, how badly can you feel wearing all sparkly rhinestones? Makes you sit up a little bit taller and hold your head up high.

The Sweet Potato Queens have made tiara wearing into a national craze and, if you need to buy one, they are kind enough to sell them on their web site. Even if you already have your very own tiara, their web site is something to behold. I suggest you pay them a visit. Even on your bleakest day, they will make you smile, if not laugh out loud. They also have plenty of good advice such as, "Never wear panties to a party." But I'll let you see that for yourself. You can find them at www.sweetpotatoqueens.com. They are well worth the visit.

GLOSSARY

Arnold
Arnold Schwarzenegger
As Happy as Larry
Drunk
Battle Dress
Business attire
Bitch
Female or gay male in need of a personality adjustment. Jack Nicholson is quoted as having said, "My mother never realized the irony of calling me a son of a bitch."
Boss
Anyone over you on the organizational chart
Boy
Male who is 18 or under, either chronologically or maturationally
Boyfriend
Male to spend uncommitted time with - try to get a man
Boy Toy
A male you are romantically involved with who is at least ten years younger than you. See also: Love Child
Career
Work for which you receive monetary compensation
Child
1. Anyone you have given birth to, adopted, or had any role in their raising, regardless of their age
2. An adult with maturity problems
Chernobyl
1. Site of a nuclear plant explosion where many were killed or injured
2. A situation that has whirled so far out of control all you can do is run for cover

Control
The illusion that your words and actions will have an immediate and lasting impact on the behavior of one or more people you are trying to influence. Something well worth striving for but, if achieved, generally found to be a temporary condition.

Date
Time spent with a man without any of his friends coming along, preferably without the television

Disconnect
Despite your best efforts, there are times when an unanticpated event occurs, screwing up your best laid plans

Divorce
End of any long term relationship

Exhaustive Research
Discussed at length with at least four of my friends

Failure
A concept that we will never recognize, much less accept

Free Time
The convergence of events when your children are happy, there is nothing your partner needs or wants, you are completely caught up at work, your house looks great, the frig is filled, dishes and laundry are done. In other words, it is strictly a concept, much like infinity. Scientists claim it exists and although you have no way to disprove it, you have no personal knowledge of it. As a matter of fact, you can't even conceptualize it.

Generally Accepted
Agreed upon by at least three of my friends and me

Girl
Always a female and depending on where you are geographically it may or may not be an indicator of age

Guidelines
Formalized list of advice shared by friends with the intention of preventing their pain or public humiliation
House
Any dwelling where you live
Husband
Male to spend committed time with - state involvement
International Research
Research conducted in more than one country
Lady
1. Female who has been schooled in deportment & proper etiquette
2. Female prisoner - thanks to Jean Harris
Love Child
A male you are romantically involved with who is at least ten years younger than you. Also see: Boy Toy
Majority Opinion
My opinion and that of at least five of my close friends. See Most People
Man
Male who has matured past adolescence
Most People
At least five of my close friends and me
Multigenerational Research
Included some youngins in my research
Old
Anyone older than 95. This is subject to change.
Pondered Extensively
Thought about for two or more days
Remedies
Methods we employ to help our friends and ourselves heal
Road Trip
Anytime you leave your house with a mission in mind; it is not necessary to leave your zip code

Road Warrior
Anyone who spends time on the road for any reason other than pleasure. Often associated with career travel but also observed in people who's children play on traveling sports teams.

Rules
Advice given by friends and not to be ignored. Use rules only for the most serious situations. For those where the consequences are not so grave, use guidelines and tips.

Sleep
A state of rest and replenishment that you never realize the value of until you are deprived of it

Sleep Deprivation
A condition where you are denied sleep; often experienced in mothers and prisoners of war

Slut
Anyone I don't like who has had sex with my husband or any of my friends' husbands - ever

Spouse
Committed partner

Spousal Equivilent
Male or female to spend committed time with - no state involvement

Tips
Advice shared by friends; generally learned the hard way

Universal Phenomena
Something experienced by the majority of my friends and me

Well Known Fact
Something agreed upon by several of my friends and me

Woman
Female older than 21; generally not southern

Youngin'
Anyone younger than I am

APPENDIX

• The Yin and the Yang •

• Communication •

• Men-Think •

The Yin
and
The Yang

HER VERSION/HIS VERSION

Her Version:

He was in an odd mood when I got to the bar, and I thought it might have been because I was a bit late. But he didn't say anything much about it and was just sort of staring off into space, so I didn't make an issue of it.

The conversation was quite slow going so I thought we should go off somewhere more intimate so we could talk more privately. We went to this restaurant and he was STILL acting a bit funny. I tried to cheer him up and started to wonder whether it was me or something else. I asked him, and he said no. But, God, he was so far removed from me! It's just so frustrating to see him go into a shell like this.

But I wasn't really sure. Could it be something I've done? So anyway, in the cab on the way back to his house, I said that I love him and he just put his arm around me. I didn't know what the hell that meant because you know he doesn't say it back or anything.

We finally got back to his place and I was wondering if he was going to dump me! So I tried to ask him about it but he just switched on the TV. Reluctantly, I said I was going to go to sleep. Then after about 10 minutes, he joined me and we had sex. But, he still seemed really distracted, so afterwards I just wanted to leave but I just cried myself to sleep instead. I dunno, I just don't know what he thinks anymore. I mean, do you think he's met someone else???

His Version:

Bruins lost. Felt tired. Got laid though.

MEN THIS/WOMEN THAT

Relationships:

First of all, a man does not call a relationship a relationship — he refers to it as "that time when me and Suzie were doing it on a semi-regular basis".

When a relationship ends, a woman will cry and pour her heart out to her girlfriends, and she will write a poem titled "All Men Are Idiots". Then she will get on with her life.

A man has a little more trouble letting go. Six months after the break-up, at 3:00 a.m. on a Saturday night, he will call and say, "I just wanted to let you know you ruined my life, and I'll never forgive you, and I hate you, and you're a total floozy. But I want you to know that there's always a chance for us". This is known as the "I Hate You / I Love You" drunken phone call, that 99% of all men have made at least once. There are community colleges that offer courses to help men get over this need; alas, these classes rarely prove effective.

Sex:

Women prefer 30-40 minutes of foreplay.

Men prefer 30-40 seconds of foreplay. Men consider driving back to her place as part of the foreplay.

Maturity:

Women mature much faster than men. Most 17-year-old females can function as adults.

Most 17-year-old males are still trading baseball cards and giving each other wedgies after gym class. This is why high school romances rarely work out.

Magazines:
Men's magazines often feature pictures of naked women.

Women's magazines also feature pictures of naked women. This is because the female body is a beautiful work of art, while the male body is lumpy and hairy and should not be seen by the light of day.

Men are turned on at the sight of a naked woman's body.

Most naked men elicit laughter from women.

Handwriting:
To their credit, men do not decorate their penmanship. They just chicken-scratch.

Women use scented colored stationary and they dot their "i's" with circles and hearts. Women use ridiculously large loops in their "p's" and "g's". It is a royal pain to read a note from a woman. Even when she's dumping you, she'll put a smiley face at the end of the note.

Comedy:
Let's say a small group of men and women are in a room, watching television, and an episode of the Three Stooges comes on. Immediately, the men will get very excited; they will laugh uproariously, and even try to imitate the actions of Curly, man's favorite Stooge.

The woman will roll their eyes and groan and wait it out.

Bathrooms:
A man has six items in his bathroom - a toothbrush, tooth-paste, shaving cream, razor, bar of Dial soap, and a towel from the Holiday Inn.

The average number of items in the typical woman's

bathroom is 437. A man would not be able to identify most of these items.

Groceries:

A woman makes a list of things she needs and then goes to the store and buys these things.

A man waits till the only items left in his fridge are half a lime and a beer. Then he goes grocery shopping. He buys everything that looks good. By the time a man reached the checkout counter, his cart is packed tighter that the Clampett's car on Beverly Hillbillies. Of course, this will not stop him from going to the 10-items-or-less lane.

Shoes:

When preparing for work, a woman will put on a Mondi wool suit, and then slip on Reebok sneakers. She will carry her dress shoes in a plastic bag from Saks. When a woman gets to work, she will put on her dress shoes. Five minutes later she will kick them off because her feet are under the desk.

A man will wear the same pair of shoes all day.

Leg Warmers:

Leg warmers are sexy. A woman, even if she's walking the dog or doing the dishes, is allowed to wear leg warmers. She can wear them any time she wants.

A man can only wear leg warmers if he is auditioning for the "Gimme the Ball" number in *A Chorus Line*.

Going Out:

When a man says he is ready to go out, it means he is ready to go out.

When a woman says she is ready to go out, it means she

WILL be ready to go out, as soon as she finds her earring, finishes putting on her makeup.

Cats:
Women love cats.

Men say they love cats, but when women aren't looking, men kick cats.

Offspring:
Ah, children. A woman knows all about her children. She knows about dentist appointments and soccer games and romances and best friends and favorite foods and secret fears and hopes and dreams.

A man is vaguely aware of some short people living in the house.

Low Blows:
Let's say a man and woman are watching a boxing match on TV. One of the boxers is felled by a low blow. The woman says "Oh, gee. That must have hurt."

The man groans and doubles over, and actually FEELS the pain.

Dressing Up:
A woman will dress up to: go shopping, water the plants, empty the garbage, answer the phone, read a book, get the mail.

A man will dress up for: weddings, funerals.

David Letterman:
Men think David Letterman is the funniest man on the face of the Earth.

Women think he is a mean, semi-dorky guy who always has a bad haircut.

Laundry:
Women do laundry every couple of days.

A man will wear every article of clothing he owns, including his surgical pants that were hip about twelve years ago, before he will do his laundry. When he is finally out of clothes, he will wear a dirty sweatshirt inside out, rent a U-Haul and take his mountain of clothes to the laundromat. Men always expect to meet beautiful women at the laundromat. This is a myth perpetuated by re-runs of old episodes of *Love, American Style*.

Weddings:
When reminiscing about weddings, women talk about "the ceremony".

Men talk about "the bachelor party".

Socks:
Men wear sensible socks. They wear standard white sweat socks.

Women wear strange socks. Socks that are cut way below the ankles, that have pictures of clouds on them, that have a big fuzzy ball on the back.

Nicknames:
If Gloria, Suzanne, Deborah and Michelle get together for lunch, they will call each other Gloria, Suzanne, Deborah and Michelle.

But if Mike, Dave, Rob and Jack go out for a brewsky, they will affectionately refer to each other as Bullet-Head,

Godzilla, Peanut-Brain and Useless.

Eating Out:
. . .and when the check comes, Mike, Dave, Rob and Jack will each throw in $20 bills, even though it's only for $22.50. None of them will have anything smaller, and none will actually admit they want change back.

When the girls get their check, out come the pocket calculators.

Mirrors:
Men are vain; they will always check themselves out in a mirror.

Women are ridiculous; they will check out their reflections in any shiny surface: mirrors , spoons, store windows, toasters, Joe Garagiola's head.

Menopause:
When a woman reaches menopause, she goes through a variety of complicated emotional, psychological, and biological changes. The nature and degree of these changes varies with the individual.

Menopause in a man provokes a uniform reaction — he buys aviator glasses, a snazzy French cap and leather driving gloves, and goes shopping for a Porsche.

The Telephone:
Men see the telephone as a communication tool. They use the telephone to send short messages to other people.

A woman can visit her girlfriend for two weeks , and upon returning home, she will call the same friend and they will talk for three hours.

Directions:
If a woman is out driving, and she finds herself in unfamiliar surroundings, she will stop at a gas station and ask for directions. Men consider this to be a sign of weakness. Men will never stop and ask for directions. Men will drive in a circle for hours, all the while saying things like, "Looks like I've found a new way to get there." and, "I know I'm in the general neighborhood. I recognize that 7-11 store."

Admitting Mistakes:
Women will sometimes admit making a mistake.

The last man who admitted he was wrong was General George Custer.

Richard Gere:
Women like Richard Gere because he is sexy in a dangerous way.

Men hate Richard Gere because he reminds them of that slick guy who works at the health club and dates only married women.

Madonna:
Same as above, but reversed. Same reason.

Toys:
Little girls love to play with toys. Then when they reach the age of 11 or 12, they lose interest.

Men never grow out of their obsession with toys. As they get older, their toys simply become more expensive and silly and impractical. Examples of men's toys: little miniature TV's. Car phones. Complicated juicers and blenders. Graphic equalizers. Small robots that serve cocktails on command. Video games. Anything that blinks, beeps, and requires at least 6 "D" batteries to operate.

Plants:
A woman asks a man to water her plants while she is on vacation.

The man waters the plants. The woman comes home five or six days later to an apartment full of dead plants. No one knows why this happens.

Cameras:
Men take photography very seriously. They'll shell out $4000, for state of the art equipment, and build dark rooms and take photography classes.

Women purchase Kodak Instamatics. Of course women always end up taking better pictures.

Garages:
Women use garages to park their cars and store their lawn-mowers.

Men use garages for many things. They hang license plates in garages, they watch TV in garages, and they build useless lopsided benches in garages.

Nudity in Movies:
Every actress in the history of movies has had to do a nude scene. This is because every movie in the history of movies has been produced by a man.

The only actor who has ever appeared nude in the movies is Richard Gere. This is another reason why men hate him.

Jewelry:
Women look nice when they wear jewelry.

A man can get away with wearing one ring and that's it. Any more than that and he will look like a lounge singer named Vic.

Movies:
For women, their favorite movie scene is when Clark Gable kisses Vivien Leigh for the first time in *Gone With The Wind*.

For men, it's when Jimmy Cagney shoves a grapefruit in Mae Clark's face in *Public Enemy*.

VIEWS ON MEN & WOMEN

Men get laid, but women get screwed.
—Quentin Crisp (English writer)

When a man goes on a date he wonders if he is going to get lucky. A woman already knows.
—Frederick Ryder

Women need a reason to have sex-men just need a place.
—Billy Crystal.

I love the lines the men use to get us into bed. "Please, I'll only put it in for a minute." What am I, a microwave?
—Beverly Mickins

Do you know why God withheld the sense of humor from women? So that we may love you instead of laugh at you.
—Mrs. Patrick Campbell

A woman's appetite is twice that of a man's; her sexual desire, four times; her intelligence, eight times.
—Sanskrit proverb

We got new advice as to what motivated man to walk upright: to free his hands for masturbation.
—Jane Wagner

March isn't the only thing that's in like a lion, out like a lamb.
—Anonymous

You know why God is a man? Because if God was a woman she would have made sperm taste like chocolate.
—Carrie Snow

Women still remember the first kiss after men have forgotten the last.
—Remy de Gourmant

A man loses his sense of direction after four drinks; a woman loses hers after four kisses.
—H.L. Mencken

When women hold off from marrying men, we call it independence. When men hold off from marrying women, we call it fear of commitment.
—Warren Farrell

Only two things are necessary to keep one's wife happy. One is to let her think she is having her own way, and the other is to let her have it.
—Lyndon B. Johnson

Why get married and make one man miserable when I can stay single and make thousands miserable?
—Carrie Snow

God made man before woman to give him time to think of an answer for her first question.
—Anonymous

GREAT QUOTES

Note from author: I have no idea whether or not any of these people actually said any of these things attributed to them. I received this on the Internet but, they go so far to illustrate my point, I have decided to share them, with the caveat that they may or may not have actually been said.

"Women might be able to fake orgasms. But men can fake whole relationships."
Sharon Stone

Honesty is the key to a relationship. If you can fake that, you're in."
Courtney Cox Monica on "Friends"

Ah, yes, divorce. . ., from the Latin word meaning to rip out a man's genitals through his wallet.
Robin Williams

Instead of getting married again, I'm going to find a woman I don't like and just give her a house.
Willie Nelson

"On the one hand, we'll never experience childbirth. On the other hand, we can open all our own jars."
Bruce Willis (On the difference between men and women)

"Luge strategy? Lie flat and try not to die."
Carmen Boyle (Olympic Luge Gold Medal winner - 1996)

Women complain about premenstrual syndrome, but I think of it as the only time of the month that I can be myself.
Roseanne

According to a new survey, women say they feel more comfortable undressing in front of men than they do undressing in front of other women. They say that women are too judgmental, whereas, of course, men are just grateful.
Robert De Niro

In the last couple of weeks I have seen the ads for the Wonder Bra. Is that really a problem in this country? Men not paying enough attention to women's breasts?
Hugh Grant

There's a new medical crisis. Doctors are reporting that many men are having allergic reactions to latex condoms. They say they cause severe swelling. So what's the problem?
Dustin Hoffman

When the sun comes up, I have morals again.
Elizabeth Taylor

There's very little advice in men's magazines, because men think, "I know what I'm doing. Just show me somebody naked."
Jerry Seinfield

See, the problem is that God gives men a brain and a penis, and only enough blood to run one at a time.
Robin Williams

Communication

BATTLE OF THE SEXES

What Women **S**ay. . . .What They **M**ean.

S   Can't we just be friends?
M   There's no way in hell I'm going to let any part of your body touch any part of mine (again).

S   I just need some space
M   without you in it.

S   Can you help me with my homework?
M   If I keep whining, the fool will do it for me.

S   Do I look fat in this dress?
M   We haven't had a fight in a while.

S   No, pizza's fine.
M   Cheap bastard.

S   I just don't want a boyfriend now
M   I just don't want (you as) a boyfriend now.

S   Don't know; what do you want to do?
M   Can't believe you have nothing planned.

S   You never listen.
M   You never listen.

S   We're moving too quickly.
M   I'm not going to sleep with you until I find out if this guy in Bio has a girlfriend.

S   I'll be ready in a minute.
M   I AM ready, but I'm going to make you wait because I know you will.

S   Oh, no, I'll pay.
M   I'm just being nice; there's no way I'm going dutch.

S   Oh, yeah... right there...
M   Well, near there; I just want to get this over with.

S   I'm just going out with the girls.
M   We're gonna get sloppy and make fun of you and your friends.

S   There's no one else.
M   I'm doing your brother.

S   Size doesn't count...
M   unless I want an orgasm.

The Other Side

S   It's just orange juice, try it.
M   3 more shots, and she'll have her legs wrapped around my head.

S   She's kind of cute.
M   I want to bang her 'till I'm blue.

S   I don't know if I like her.
M   She won't blow me.

S	I need you.
M	My hand is tired.

S	I had her.
M	I had (wet dreams about) her.

S	I really want to get to know you better
M	...so I can tell my friends about it.

S	How do I compare with all your other boyfriends?
M	Is my penis really that small?

S	You're the only girl I've ever cared about.
M	You're the only girl who hasn't rejected me this year.

S	I want you back.
M	. . .for tonight, anyway.

S	We've been through so much together.
M	If it wasn't for you, I never would have lost my virginity.

S	I miss you so much.
M	I'm so horny that my roommate is starting to look good.

S	I don't think I want to dance right now.
M	Shit! She'll know I have a hard-on.

S	The break-up shouldn't start 'till tomorrow.
M	I want to have sex with you a few more times.

Men Think

THE MALE SPECIES

These are **THEIR** Rules and Guidelines:

• Any Man who brings a camera to a stag night may be legally killed or beaten by his fellow partygoers.

• Under no circumstances may two men share an umbrella.

• It is OK for a man to cry under the following circumstances:

a. When a heroic dog dies to save his master
b. The moment Angelina Jolie starts unbuttoning her blouse
c. After wrecking your boss' car
d. One hour, 12 minutes, 37 seconds into "The Crying Game"
e. When his date is using her teeth

• Unless he murdered someone in your family, you must bail a friend out of jail within 12 hours.

• If you've known a guy for more than 24 hours, his sister is off limits forever, unless you actually marry her. (Whoops)

• The minimum amount of time you have to wait for a guy who's running late is 5 minutes. Maximum waiting time is 6 minutes. For a girl, you have to wait 10 minutes for every point of hotness she scores on the classic 1-10 scale.

• Bitching about the brand of free beer in a friend's fridge is forbidden. Gripe at will if the temperature is unsuitable.

• No man shall ever be required to buy a birthday present for another man. In fact, even remembering your buddies birthday is optional.

• When stumbling upon other guys watching a sporting event, you may always ask the score of the game in progress, but you may never ask who's playing.

• It is permissible to quaff a fruity chick drink only when you're sunning on a tropical beach. . .and it's delivered by a topless supermodel. . .and it's free.

• Computers let you make more mistakes faster than any other invention in human history, with the possible exceptions of handguns and tequila.

• Friends don't let friends wear Speedos. Ever. Issue closed.

• If a man's zipper is down, that's his problem-you didn't see nothin'.

• Women who claim they "love to watch sports" must be treated as spies until they demonstrate knowledge of the game and the ability to drink as much beer as the other sports watchers.

• You must offer heartfelt and public condolences over the death of a girlfriend's cat, even if it was you who secretly threw it into a ceiling fan.

• Never hesitate to reach for the last beer or the last slice of pizza, but not both. That's just plain mean.

• Never talk to a man in a bathroom unless you are on equal footing: both urinating, both waiting in line, etc. For all other situations, an almost imperceptible nod is all the conversation you need.

• Never allow a conversation with a woman to go on longer than you are able to have sex with her. Keep a stopwatch by the phone; Hang up if necessary.

• The morning after you and a babe who was formerly "just a friend" have had carnal drunken rampant sex, the fact that you're feeling weird and guilty is no reason not to do it again before the discussion about what a big mistake it was.

Ten Things Men Know About Women:

1.

2.

3.

4.

5.

6.

7.

8.

9.

10. They have boobs

Why It's Great to Be a Guy:

-Your ass is never a factor in a job interview.
-Your orgasms are real. Always.
-The garage is all yours.
-Nobody secretly wonders if you swallow.
-Wedding plans take care of themselves.
-Chocolate is just another snack.
-You can be president.
-You can wear a white shirt to a water park.
-Foreplay is optional.
-You never feel compelled to stop a friend from getting laid.
-Car mechanics tell you the truth.
-You don't give a rat's ass if someone notices your new haircut.
-The world is your urinal.
-Hot wax never comes near your pubic area.
-You never have to drive to another gas station because this one's just too icky
-Same work. . .more pay.
-You don't have to leave the room to make emergency crotch adjustments.
-If you retain water, it's in a canteen.
-People never glance at your chest when you're talking to them.
-Princess Di's death was just another obituary.
-New shoes don't cut, blister, or mangle your feet.
-Porn movies are designed with you in mind.
-Not liking a person does not preclude having great sex with them.
-Your pals can be trusted never to trap you with: "So, notice anything different?"
-Phone conversations last 30 seconds
-You know useful stuff about tanks and airplanes
-A 5-day vacation requires only one suitcase

-Bathroom lines are 80% shorter
-You can open all your own jars
-Old friends don't care if you've lost or gained weight
-When clicking through the channels you don't have to stop
 on every shot of someone crying
-You don't have to lug a bag of "necessary" items with you
 everywhere you go
-You can go to the bathroom alone
-Your last name stays put
-You can leave a hotel room bed unmade
-You can kill your own food
-You get extra credit for the slightest act of thoughtfulness
-You see the humor in "Terms of Endearment"
-Cleaning the toilet is optional
-You can be showered and ready in 10 minutes
-If someone forgets to invite you to something, they can still
 be your friend
-Your underwear costs $7.50 for a pack of 3
-None of your coworkers have the power to make you cry
-You don't have to shave below your neck
-You don't have to curl up next to some big, hairy guy every
 night
-If you're 34 and single, no one notices
-You can quietly enjoy a car ride from the passenger seat
-Flowers and/or Duct Tape fix everything
-You never have to worry about other's feelings
-Three pair of shoes are more than enough
-You can say anything and not worry about what people think
-You can whip your shirt off on a hot day
-You can watch a game in silence for hours without your
 buddy thinking "He must be mad at me"
-You can admire Clint Eastwood without having to starve
 yourself to look like him
-Gray hair and wrinkles add character

-Wedding dress $2000, Tux rental $100 bucks
-You don't care if someone is talking behind your back
-You don't pass on the dessert and then mooch off someone
 else's
-The remote is yours and yours alone
-You need not pretend you're "freshening up" when you go to
 the bathroom
-If you don't call your buddy when you said you would, he
 won't tell your friends you've changed
-If another guy shows up at the party in the same outfit, you
 might become lifelong buddies
-The occasional well-rendered belch is practically expected
-If something mechanical didn't work, you can bash it with a
 hammer and throw it across the room
-One mood, all the time - horny.

Test for Men:

Here's some insight to the male world (as if we couldn't predict the answers ourselves!!).

1. Alien beings from a highly advanced society visit the Earth, and you are the first human they encounter. As a token of intergalactic friendship, they present you with a small but incredibly sophisticated device that is capable of curing all disease, providing an infinite supply of clean energy, wiping out hunger and poverty, and permanently eliminating oppression and violence all over the entire Earth. You decide to:

    A. Present it to the President of the United States.
    B. Present it to the Secretary General of the United Nations.
    C. Take it apart.

2. As you grow older, what lost quality of your youthful life do you miss the most?

    A. Innocence.
    B. Idealism.
    C. Cherry bombs.

3. When is it okay to kiss another male?

    A. When you wish to display simple and pure affection without regard for narrow-minded social conventions.
    B. When he is the Pope. (Not on the lips.)
    C. When he is your brother and you are Al Pacino and this is the only really sportsman-like way to let him know that, for business reasons, you have to have him killed.

4. What about hugging another male?

    A. If he's your father and at least one of you has a fatal di ease.
    B. If you're performing the Heimlich Maneuver.
    C. If you're a professional baseball player and a teammate hits a homerun to win the World Series, you may hug him, provided that:
        (1) He is legally within the base path,
        (2) Both of you are wearing sufficient protection, and
        (3) You also pound him fraternally with your fist hard enough to cause fractures.

5. In your opinion, the ideal pet is:

    A. A cat.
    B. A dog.
    C. A dog that eats cats.

6. You have been seeing a woman for several years. She's attractive and intelligent, and you always enjoy being with her. One leisurely Sunday afternoon the two of you are taking it easy - you're watching a football game; she's reading the paper - when she suddenly, out of the clear blue sky, tells you that she thinks she really loves you, but, she can no longer bear the uncertainty of not knowing where your relationship is going. She says she's not asking whether you want to get married; only whether you believe that you have some kind of future together. What do you say?

    A. That you sincerely believe the two of you do have a future, but you don't want to rush it.
    B. That although you also have strong feelings for her, you cannot honestly say that you'll be ready anytime soon to make a lasting commitment, and you don't want to hurt her

by holding out false hope.

C. That you cannot believe the Jets called a draw play on third and seventeen.

7. Okay, so you have decided that you truly love a woman and you want to spend the rest of your life with her - sharing the joys and the sorrows, the world has to offer, come what may. How do you tell her?

A. You take her to a nice restaurant and tell her after dinner.
B. You take her for a walk on a moonlit beach, and you say her name, and when she turns to you, with the sea breeze blowing her hair and the stars in her eyes, you tell her.
C. Tell her what?

8. One weekday morning your wife wakes up feeling ill and asks you to get your three children ready for school. Your first question to her is:

A. "Do they need to eat or anything?"
B. "They're in school already?"
C. "There are three of them?"

9. When is it okay to throw away a set of veteran underwear?

A. When it has turned the color of a dead whale and developed new holes so large that you're not sure which ones were originally intended for your legs.
B. When it is down to eight loosely connected underwear molecules and had to be handled with tweezers.
C. It is never okay to throw away veteran underwear. A real guy checks the garbage regularly in case somebody-and we are not naming names, but this would be his wife-is quietly trying to discard his underwear, which she is frankly jealous

of, because the guy seems to have a more intimate relation
ship with it than with her.

10. What, in your opinion, is the most reasonable
explanation for the fact that Moses led the Israelites all over
the place for forty years before they finally got to the
Promised Land?

    A. He was being tested.
    B. He wanted them to really appreciate the Promised Land
       when they finally got there.
    C. He refused to ask for directions.

11. What is the human race's single greatest achievement?

    A. Democracy.
    B. Religion.
    C. Remote control.

**Note:* All "real men" answer "C" to all of these questions.
Know this, and you will have come far in understanding men
and enriching your own life.*

THESE ARE THEIR HEROS

Oiler coach Bum Phillips: When asked by Bob Costas why he takes his wife on all the road trips, Phillips responded, *"Because she is too damn ugly to kiss good-bye."*

Chicago Cubs outfielder Andre Dawson on being a role model: *"I want all the kids to do what I do, to look up to me. I want all the kids to copulate me."*

New Orleans Saint RB George Rogers when asked about the upcoming season: *"I want to rush for 1,000 or 1,500 yards, whichever comes first."*

And, upon hearing Joe Jacoby of the 'Skins say *"I'd run over my own mother to win the Super Bowl,"* Matt Millen of the Raiders said, *"to win, I'd run over Joe's Mom too."*

Football commentator and former player Joe Theismann 1996: *"Nobody in football should be called a genius. A genius is guy like Norman Einstein."*

Senior basketball player at the University of Pittsburgh: *"I'm going to graduate on time, no matter how long it takes".*

Bill Peterson, a Florida State football coach: *"You guys line up alphabetically by height."* and *"You guys pair up in groups of three, then line up in a circle."*

Clemson recruit Ray Forsythe, who was ineligible as a freshman because of academic requirements: *"I play football. I'm not trying to be a professor. The tests don't seem to make sense to me, measuring your brain on stuff I haven't been through in school."*

Boxing promoter Dan Duva on Mike Tyson hooking up again with promoter Don King: *"Why would anyone expect him to come out smarter? He went to prison for 3 years, not Princeton."*

Stu Grimson, Chicago Blackhawks left wing, explaining why he keeps a color photo of himself above his locker: *"That's so when I forget how to spell my name, I can still find my @#%#%@ clothes."*

Shaquille O'Neal on whether he had visited the Parthenon during his visit to Greece: *"I can't really remember the names of the clubs that we went to."*

Lou Duva, veteran boxing trainer, on the Spartan training regime of heavyweight Andrew Golota: *"He's a guy who gets up at six o'clock in the morning regardless of what time it is."*

Pat Williams, Orlando Magic general manager, on his team's 7-27 record: *"We can't win at home. We can't win on the road. As general manager, I just can't figure out where else to play."* (1992)

Chuck Nevitt, North Carolina State basketball player, explaining to Coach Jim Valvano why he appeared nervous at practice: *"My sister's expecting a baby, and I don't know if I'm going to be an uncle or an aunt."* (1982)

Tommy Lasorda, Dodger manager, when asked what terms Mexican-born pitching sensation Fernando Valenzuela might settle for in his upcoming contract negotiations: *"He wants Texas back."* (1981)

Darrell Royal, Texas football coach, asked if the abnormal number of Longhorn injuries that season resulted from poor physical conditioning: *"One player was lost because he broke his nose. How do you go about getting a nose in condition for football?"* (1966)

Mike McCormack, coach of the hapless Baltimore Colts after the team's co-captain, offensive guard Robert Pratt, pulled a hamstring running onto the field for the coin toss against St. Louis: *"I'm going to send the injured reserve players out for the toss next time."* (1981)

Steve Spurrier, Florida football coach, telling Gator fans that a fire at Auburn's football dorm had destroyed 20 books: *"But the real tragedy was that 15 hadn't been colored yet."* (1991)

Jim Finks, New Orleans Saints GM, when asked after a loss what he thought of the refs: *"I'm not allowed to comment on lousy officiating."* (1986)

Alan Kulwicki, stock car racer, on racing Saturday nights as opposed to Sunday afternoons: *"It's basically the same, just darker."* (1991)

Lincoln Kennedy, Oakland Raiders tackle, on his decision not to vote: *"I was going to write myself in, but I was afraid I'd get shot."* (1996)

Frank Layden, Utah Jazz president, on a former player: *"I told him, 'Son, what is it with you. Is it ignorance or apathy?' He said, 'Coach, I don't know and I don't care.' "* (1991)

Torrin Polk, University of Houston receiver, on his coach, John Jenkins: *"He treats us like men. He lets us wear earrings."* (1991)

Shelby Metcalf, basketball coach at Texas A&M, recounting what he told a player who received four F's and one D: *"Son, looks to me like you're spending too much time on one subject."* (1987)

Attributed to one of the all-time baseball flakes, Joaquin Andujar: *"In baseball, it all comes down to one word: You never know."*

Another from former major league infielder, Tito Fuentes, after being hit by a pitch: *"They shouldn't throw at me. I'm the father of five or six kids."*

To Order:

the working woman's guide to
BALANCING KIDS, CAREER, HOUSE AND SPOUSE

$14.95 plus $3.50 Shipping & Handling
Payable by Visa, Mastercard or Check

Bill My: ❑ Visa ❑ MasterCard ❑ Check

Card #: _____ Expires: _____

Signature: _____

Name: _____

Address: _____

State: _____ Zip: _____

Phone: _____

Mail To:

Gráinne Enterprises
P.O. Box 1505, Manchester, MA 01944
Phone: 978-526-4183 • Fax: 978-526-4193

Web Site: www.mimi-obara.com
E-mail: mimi@mimi-obara.com